D1157994

Energy Alternatives

by Karen D. Povey

LUCENT BOOKS

An imprint of Thomson Gale, a part of The Thomson Corporation

Detroit • New York • San Francisco • New Haven, Conn. • Waterville, Maine • London

© 2007 Thomson Gale, a part of The Thomson Corporation.

Thomson and Star Logo are trademarks and Gale and Lucent Books are registered trademarks used herein under license.

For more information, contact
Lucent Books
27500 Drake Rd.
Farmington Hills, MI 48331-3535
Or you can visit our Internet site at http://www.gale.com

ALL RIGHTS RESERVED.
No part of this work covered by the copyright hereon may be reproduced or used in any form or by any means—graphic, electronic, or mechanical, including photocopying, recording, taping, Web distribution, or information storage retrieval systems—without the written permission of the publisher.

Every effort has been made to trace the owners of copyrighted material.

LIBRARY OF CONGRESS CATALOGING-IN-PUBLICATION DATA

Povey, Karen D., 1962–
  Energy alternatives / by Karen D. Povey.
    p. cm. — (Hot topics)
  Includes bibliographical references and index.
  ISBN 978-1-59018-980-1 (hardcover)
  1. Renewable energy sources—Juvenile literature. 2. Power resources—Juvenile literature. I. Title.
  TJ808.2.P68 2007
  333.79—dc22

2007007782

ISBN-10: 1-59018-980-9

Printed in the United States of America

CONTENTS

FOREWORD

Young people today are bombarded with information. Aside from traditional sources such as newspapers, television, and the radio, they are inundated with a nearly continuous stream of data from electronic media. They send and receive e-mails and instant messages, read and write online "blogs," participate in chat rooms and forums, and surf the Web for hours. This trend is likely to continue. As Patricia Senn Breivik, the dean of university libraries at Wayne State University in Detroit, states, "Information overload will only increase in the future. By 2020, for example, the available body of information is expected to double every 73 days! How will these students find the information they need in this coming tidal wave of information?"

Ironically, this overabundance of information can actually impede efforts to understand complex issues. Whether the topic is abortion, the death penalty, gay rights, or obesity, the deluge of fact and opinion that floods the print and electronic media is overwhelming. The news media report the results of polls and studies that contradict one another. Cable news shows, talk radio programs, and newspaper editorials promote narrow viewpoints and omit facts that challenge their own political biases. The World Wide Web is an electronic minefield where legitimate scholars compete with the postings of ordinary citizens who may or may not be well-informed or capable of reasoned argument. At times, strongly worded testimonials and opinion pieces both in print and electronic media are presented as factual accounts.

Conflicting quotes and statistics can confuse even the most diligent researchers. A good example of this is the question of whether or not the death penalty deters crime. For instance, one study found that murders decreased by nearly one-third when the death penalty was reinstated in New York in 1995. Death penalty supporters cite this finding to support their argument that the existence of the death penalty deters criminals from committing murder. However, another study found that states without the death penalty have murder rates below the national average. This study is cited by opponents of capital punishment, who reject the claim that the death penalty deters murder. Students need context and clear, informed discussion if they are to think critically and make informed decisions.

The Hot Topics series is designed to help young people wade through the glut of fact, opinion, and rhetoric so that they can think critically about controversial issues. Only by reading and thinking critically will they be able to formulate a viewpoint that is not simply the parroted views of others. Each volume of the series focuses on one of today's most pressing social issues and provides a balanced overview of the topic. Carefully crafted narrative, fully documented primary and secondary source quotes, informative sidebars, and study questions all provide excellent starting points for research and discussion. Full-color photographs and charts enhance all volumes in the series. With its many useful features, the Hot Topics series is a valuable resource for young people struggling to understand the pressing issues of the modern era.

INTRODUCTION

ADDICTED TO OIL

When President George W. Bush proclaimed that "America is addicted to oil"[1] during his 2006 State of the Union address, he prompted a new national discussion of one of the country's most critical issues. Although Americans represent only 5 percent of the world's population, they consume 25 percent of the world's oil production, mostly in the form of vehicle fuel. This consumption shows no sign of letting up; each year Americans use even more oil than the year before.

Although Americans are the leaders in global energy use, the rest of the world is showing signs of catching up. Growth in the populations and economies of China and India put them on course to rival the United States' energy use in the future. The global rate of oil consumption—some 84 million barrels a day and growing—will not be sustainable forever. Although experts debate how much oil remains, all agree that it will eventually run out.

Kicking the Fossil Fuel Habit

As Americans become aware of the need to find alternatives to oil to provide energy for all the activities of daily life, there are fears that this awareness may be too late. Even with a new call to action, many industry experts believe there may not be time to ramp up technology quickly enough to support energy alternatives by the time fossil fuels begin to run dry.

Despite fears that alternatives have been slow to catch on, many new energy technologies are gaining momentum, slowly eating away at fossil fuels' energy dominance. These renewable energy sources, such as wind, solar, and geothermal power, are growing at rates of from 20 to 60 percent each year. If this growth continues, optimistic estimates show that it may be possible for renewable energy to account for half of the world's energy use by 2040.

Expanding the use of renewable energy is also considered critical for the long-term health of the planet. Fossil fuels have been responsible for a host of environmental ills from acid rain to global warming. Many environmentalists believe that kicking the fossil fuel habit before damage to the planet is irreversible should be a global priority.

James Watt's first "Sun and Planet" steam engine was developed in 1769.

Scientists have been trying to come up with alternatives to fossil fuels. Fossil fuels have been responsible for numerous problems, one of which is acid rain, which has led to the need for acid rain monitors.

The quest to develop affordable, effective alternatives to fossil fuels may be one of the most challenging technological tasks in human history. Fortunately, scientists all over the world are up to the challenge, working to uncover the next alternative energy breakthroughs. Supporting their efforts are individuals everywhere who do their part to conserve energy and limit their own use of nonrenewable fossil fuels.

IN PURSUIT OF ENERGY ALTERNATIVES

Ever since the days when ancient people huddled around their campfires, the search for energy has dominated human culture. Early hunter-gatherers could easily find wood to fuel fires for cooking and providing warmth as they wandered from place to place. However, as people began to concentrate in towns and eventually larger cities, these fuel supplies became scarce. Local forests quickly disappeared as people harvested firewood to meet their growing needs for energy. The demand for energy accelerated as early industries such as making pottery and smelting metals developed.

The Energy Economy Emerges

As forests were depleted and people were forced to venture ever farther seeking fuel, the first systems for finding and distributing energy evolved. This new "energy economy" nourished an industry that bridged the gap between the need for energy and the fuel supply. A trade in firewood developed in which wood was collected, dried, stored, and sold or traded. Firewood had

The Lucas gusher, drilled in Texas in 1901, was the first high-producing oil well.

9

become a resource that had value to both the dealer and the buyer.

At the same time, the effects of a limited supply of wood could be felt. As wood became scarce, prices rose and the threat of running out became real. This situation had a significant impact on developing societies. Author Paul Roberts explains the pattern in his book *The End of Oil*:

> In short, energy had become a strategic resource—a factor in the rise, and fall, of economies and civilizations. Catastrophic fuel shortages were probably quite frequent. Indeed, the march of human progress may well have been marked by a series of energy crises that either killed off a particular civilization or helped push it to the next level of technological and economic development.[2]

Energy shortages were especially severe in Europe. By medieval times, rapidly growing populations and new manufacturing industries were consuming vast quantities of firewood. By the fifteenth century, firewood was so expensive that only the wealthiest people could afford to buy it. As wood supplies ran out, people turned to using coal for fuel. Coal was a poor alternative to wood because it produced thick, smelly smoke that burned eyes, blackened clothing, and fouled the taste of food. Coal, however, was plentiful and cheap, and it provided much more energy than wood when burned.

The invention of the steam engine in the 1700s, however, finally allowed the benefits of coal to be realized. Engines changed the way that energy was used. Instead of just being burned to produce energy for cooking or heating, coal could now be burned to produce mechanical energy as well. This mechanical energy could do the same work that previously required the efforts of people, horses, or oxen. With so much available coal, the Industrial Revolution was fueled. Factories sprang up rapidly, using engines to power the manufacture of a multitude of products. Trains and steamships carried people and cargo throughout Europe and the United States. By 1900 nearly 1 billion tons (907 billion kg) of coal was being used each year.

Consumer Culture

In his book *The End of Oil*, author Paul Roberts examines the potential growth in energy use in the developing world.

Are the energy trends and tendencies of the United States and the rest of the postindustrial West indicative of what is to come in developing countries over the next two or three decades? Should we expect to see two-car garages, big-screen televisions, and three-quarter-ton pickup trucks in places like Rio, New Delhi, or Beijing? Will people in China and India not be satisfied until they consume as much oil, gas, and electricity as Americans do?

One could argue that America is a special case. One could insist that American consumers are unique in their energy obliviousness, or that the status of the United States as a superpower and world policemen somehow entitles Americans to worry less about energy. It may be that other countries won't follow this path, won't trade away their efficiency dividend for an energy-lavish lifestyle or yield to the escalating spiral of consumption.

Paul Roberts, *The End of Oil*. New York: Houghton Mifflin, 2004, pp.155–56.

The Rise of Oil

Although coal had replaced wood as a readily available and inexpensive source of energy, it still had its drawbacks. Coal was bulky to store and did not burn hot enough for some industrial uses. Additionally, the soot-related problems of illness and pollution remained. Coal's dominance as an energy source changed forever, however, when the first high-producing oil well was drilled in Texas in 1901. Almost immediately, oil became a favored energy source over coal due to its ability to burn cleaner, its ease of storage, and its ability to provide greater amounts of energy. However, because of its abundance and low cost, coal is still widely used, especially in the developing world.

Oil's superiority over coal became complete with the arrival of the automobile powered by the gasoline-driven internal combustion engine. Automobiles and other forms of transportation completely transformed the way that people lived. A global economy arose that was based on the oil that powered the ships, trains, cars, trucks, buses, and airplanes that moved people and products faster and farther than ever before.

Today energy—especially that produced by oil—dominates the world's modern cultures. As Paul Roberts observes, "We produce and consume energy not simply to heat and feed ourselves, to move ourselves, or to defend ourselves, but to educate and entertain ourselves, to expand our knowledge, change our destiny, construct and reconstruct our world, and fill it with stuff."[3] Just as the uses of energy have expanded, so has the demand for vehicle fuel and electricity. In the past twenty years, global energy use has risen by 50 percent. The United States Department of Energy projects that world oil demand will nearly double again by 2030.

How Much Oil Remains?

Will there be enough oil to meet this growing demand? Just as shortages of wood resources caused previous societies to turn to coal, many experts predict that oil shortages will force people to find other ways to meet the world's energy needs. Oil and other fossil fuels are nonrenewable resources that cannot be replaced once they are used up. Experts agree that eventually, alternative sources of energy will be needed to replace fossil fuels. However, there is a great deal of disagreement on the urgency of the problem.

Much of the debate about the world's remaining oil reserves focuses on the concept of peak production. Peak production is the point in time when roughly half of the world's accessible oil has been taken from the earth. After peak production is reached, oil reserves will be declining. Joe Romm, former U.S. assistant energy secretary, cautions those who see the peak as being a point midway into the world's oil supply. "The point to remember about production isn't that it peaks, but that it declines rapidly afterward, at a time when the world demand would be moving rapidly in the opposite direction." After the peak, Romm says, "there is very little time for the U.S. to react."[4] Physicist David Goodstein echoes this viewpoint. "The crisis will come not when we pump the last drop of oil, but rather when the rate at which oil can be pumped out of the ground starts to diminish."[5]

WHEN WILL THE OIL RUN OUT?

"How long will it last? No one can predict the future, but the world contains enough petroleum resources to last at least until the year 2100. This is so far in the future that it would be ludicrous for us to try to anticipate what energy sources our descendants will utilize."

—David Deming, University of Oklahoma
School of Geology and Geophysics

Quoted in Daniel A. Leone, ed., *Is the World Heading Toward an Energy Crisis?* Detroit: Greenhaven, 2006, p. 29.

In 2002 the United States Geological Survey (USGS) esti- mated that over 3 trillion barrels of recoverable oil remained, enough to keep production from peaking for another thirty- three years. Many experts disagree and believe the oil peak is close at hand or may have already passed. Although oil fields in the Persian Gulf and Russia continue to produce well, in the United States oil production peaked in 1971. Most established oil fields worldwide have declining production, and new fields are getting harder to find. New oil fields that are found are usu- ally smaller and more difficult to access. Therefore it costs more to extract the oil, and it is more expensive for consumers to buy oil products.

"We've been drilling holes all over the world since the early 1900s," says Les Magoon, a geologist with the USGS who does not share that agency's view that large oil reserves remain. "Statistically, it's unlikely that there is all this 'hidden resource,' waiting to be found," he says. "It is pretty hard to support sci- entifically."[6] Author and Princeton geologist Kenneth Deffeyes puts it another way. "Finding oil is like fishing in a pond. After several months, you notice that you are not catching as many fish. You could buy an expensive fly rod—new technology. Or you could decide that you have already caught most of the fish in the pond."[7]

The technology Deffeyes speaks of has allowed oil supplies once considered impossible to reach to have increased potential for being tapped. Oil can now be drawn out of deposits of sticky tar sands in Canada, from below frozen tundra, or from deep undersea wells. Another USGS geologist, Tom Ahlbrandt, has an optimistic opinion about these hidden oil supplies. "We feel that more than half of all undiscovered resources are in the deep offshore, of which half are in the Arctic. . . . We haven't even begun to discover all the oil that is out there."[8] As prices for oil rise, it becomes profitable for companies to spend more money to tap difficult oil sources. Kenneth Rogoff, a Harvard economist, insists, "We might be running low on $20 [per barrel] oil, but for $60 we have adequate oil supplies for decades to come."[9]

Large deposits of sticky tar sands in Alberta, Canada, can produce approximately 175 million barrels of oil.

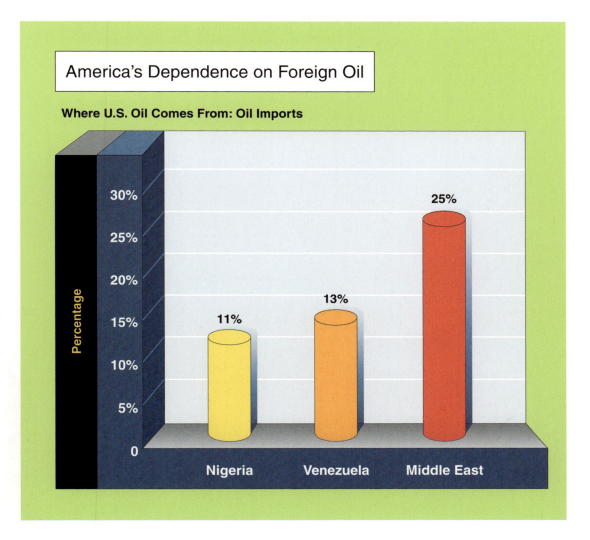

America's Dependence on Foreign Oil

Where U.S. Oil Comes From: Oil Imports

Will We Be Prepared?

It is impossible to predict when oil will run out, but perhaps that is not the most important question. Instead, the question might be, will we be prepared? Paul Roberts explains:

> Yet thus far, governments, and the populations that elect them, seem to be in a state of denial about petroleum. It is true that efforts have been made to develop alternative fuels or shift the energy economy to natural gas, but

such programs will cost trillions of dollars and require decades to carry out. Thus, the real question is not whether oil is going to run out (it will) but whether we have the capacity, the political will, to *see* that outcome soon enough to prepare ourselves for it.[10]

Surface mining by heavy machinery exposes tar sand deposits for transport in Fort McMurray, Alberta, Canada.

Preparing an energy-dependent world for a future without oil is a top concern for many people. Many experts fear, however, that progress toward alternative energy sources has been far too slow. Matt Simmons, an energy investment banker and adviser to the Bush administration, protests, "The experts and politicians have no Plan B to fall back on."[11] Although Joe Romm does not believe a peak is imminent, he shares Simmons's concern. "I am increasingly of the opinion that when it does peak, it will be too late to do anything about it."[12]

The Environmental Costs of Fossil Fuels

The threat of running out of oil is only one factor fueling the pursuit of energy alternatives. As the environmental impacts of using fossil fuels become ever more apparent, maintaining the long-term health of the planet has become a driving force for advocates of finding cleaner energy alternatives.

SUPPLIES WILL PEAK

"Peaking of oil and gas will occur, if it has not already happened, and we will never know when the event has happened until we see it 'in our rear view mirrors.'"
—Matthew Simmons, energy investment banker and adviser to the Bush administration's 2001 Energy Task Force

Quoted in Paul Roberts, *The End of Oil*. New York: Houghton Mifflin, 2004, p. 60.

Some of the environmental costs of extracting, transporting, and burning fossil fuels are visible and have been studied for decades. Reaching fossil fuels buried deep underground often requires major disturbances to natural landscapes. Most coal, for example, is removed through a process known as surface mining. In surface mining, enormous open pits are dug to expose and remove coal-bearing rock. When the coal seams are exposed to air and water, toxic chemicals are formed that can impact local soils and waterways. Although modern oil-drilling techniques have minimized the environmental damage of removing oil from underground, hazards remain when oil is transported through pipelines or by tanker ships. Oil spills such

A huge oil slick surrounds the Exxon Valdez *in 1989, where between 11 and 45 million gallons of oil is estimated to have spilled into Prince William Sound, Alaska, killing thousands of marine animals.*

as the 11 million gallons (42 million liters) spilled from the *Exxon Valdez* in Alaska in 1989 can kill thousands of marine animals and have long-lasting harmful effects on fragile ecosystems.

Although retrieving and transporting fossil fuels can cause lasting environmental damage, the most serious harm results when these fuels are burned to create energy. The exhaust from burning gasoline and diesel fuel in car engines and coal in factories and power plants creates a toxic mix of pollution. Once in the air, these pollutants, including carbon monoxide and nitrogen oxide, undergo chemical reactions to form the visible pollution known as smog. Smog can cause breathing problems such as asthma and contributes to birth defects. Smog-forming reactions occur while the pollution is blown through the air, so smog is often present in places far from its source.

Another far-reaching consequence of car and factory exhaust is acid rain. Acid rain is formed when sulfur and nitrogen released from burning coal and gasoline react with oxygen and water in the atmosphere. These chemical compounds are carried long distances on air currents, eventually falling to earth in rain and snow. Acid rain changes the pH level in lakes and streams, killing microorganisms, invertebrates, and fish. Many plants are also affected by acid rain. Huge tracts of forests in Canada, the northeastern United States, Europe, and Asia have been damaged or killed by acid rain. In China, where coal is the primary form of energy, acid rain has badly damaged nearly 40 percent of forests and farmlands.

Carbon Emissions and Climate Change

Whereas smog and the effects of acid rain are easily visible, the impact of another, potentially much greater, threat is a good deal more difficult to discern. Fossil fuels are primarily composed of the decayed remains of ancient plants and animals. Those remains hold the carbon that living plants once absorbed from the carbon dioxide in the atmosphere. When fossil fuels are burned, the carbon in the fuel combines with oxygen, forming carbon dioxide that is released back into the atmosphere. Some of this carbon dioxide is recaptured by growing plants as they absorb carbon dioxide through photosynthesis. However, carbon stores in fossil fuels are being released at a much more rapid rate than they were deposited over millions of years.

These trees in North Carolina were damaged by exposure to acid rain.

For example, in 1997 a researcher calculated that the entire human population burned the equivalent of four hundred times the total plant material grown that year. Releasing such large quantities of carbon dioxide through the burning of fossil fuels has resulted in a gradual rise in the levels of carbon dioxide in the atmosphere. In the two hundred years between the beginning of the Industrial Revolution and 2005, the concentration of carbon dioxide in the atmosphere has nearly tripled. In fact, studies of ice-core samples indicate that current carbon dioxide levels (372 parts per million of carbon dioxide in ice-core samples taken in 2005) are at their highest in at least 420,000 years.

HEATING THE EARTH LIKE A POT OF WATER

"Pump enough CO_2 [carbon dioxide] into the sky, and that last part per million of greenhouse gas behaves like the 212th degree Fahrenheit that turns a pot of hot water into a plume of billowing steam."

—Jeffrey Kluger

Jeffrey Kluger, "The Tipping Point," *Time*, April 3, 2006, p. 35.

Carbon dioxide is considered a greenhouse gas, responsible for trapping the earth's heat in the atmosphere. Scientists believe that with higher atmospheric levels of carbon dioxide, less heat will be able to escape into space, resulting in a gradual rise in the earth's temperature—a phenomenon known as global warming. When the theory of global warming was first suggested, many people dismissed it as a real possibility or significant concern. Some explained the rise in carbon dioxide levels or the earth's temperature as naturally occurring fluctuations. Many people had difficulty accepting the idea that human activity was responsible for the change.

Now, however, mounting evidence has caused most scientists, politicians, and the general public alike to accept that global warming as a result of fossil fuel emissions is taking place. Most debate now focuses instead on what the effects such an increase will have. Since 1750 the earth's average temperature has risen by 1.4°F (0.78°C). It is extremely difficult to predict how much it will

Former vice president Al Gore testifies on Capitol Hill in 2007 on the negative effects of worldwide global warming.

increase in the future. If carbon dioxide emissions continue to climb with the ever-increasing burning of fossil fuels, the rate of temperature increase is expected to accelerate. In February 2007 an international team of climate experts serving on the United Nations Intergovernmental Panel on Climate Change (IPCC) released a report that estimated a rise in global temperatures from 3.2°F to 7.8°F (1.8°C to 4.4°C) by 2100.

Even with the current small increase in temperature, environmental changes have been noted. Polar ice and glaciers worldwide are melting, birds and butterflies are shifting their ranges northward, and ocean storms are gaining strength. "There is no debate among any statured scientists working on this issue about the larger trends of what is happening to the climate,"[13] says James McCarthy, cochair of the IPCC. Many experts believe these changes are just a small taste of the environmental storm brewing. If temperatures continue to increase at an accelerated rate, entire ice sheets in Greenland and Antarctica may melt, raising global sea levels enough to swamp large parts of coastal Florida, many Pacific islands, and parts of Southeast Asia. Entire ecosystems may be altered as plants and animals either adapt or die out in response to the changing climate.

Former vice president Al Gore has long sounded the alarm about the disastrous consequences climate change may spell. "'Global warming' is the name it was given a long time ago. But it should be understood for what it is: a planetary emergency that now threatens human civilization on multiple fronts. Stronger hurricanes and typhoons represent only one of many new dangers as we begin what someone has called 'a nature hike

The Carbon Cost of Cars

Author Richard Conniff was amazed to learn that for each gallon of gas his car burned, 25 pounds (11kg) of carbon dioxide was released into the atmosphere. Since a gallon of gas weighs only about 6 pounds (2.7kg), he wondered how his fuel produced so much more pollution. To find out, Conniff did some calculations.

[Gasoline is] about 90 percent carbon. Combustion causes almost every atom of carbon in the fuel to combine with two atoms of oxygen, producing carbon dioxide. Despite our tendency to think of it as weightless, oxygen is in fact 1.33 times heavier than carbon. So the original 6 pounds of carbon combine with 15 or 16 pounds of oxygen, minus some soot, water, and other by-products, and, bingo, by driving 21 miles down the road, my car has just disturbed the balance of the planet's carbon cycle by producing 19 pounds of CO_2 [carbon dioxide]. Emissions released in manufacturing and transporting the gas to market add another 6 pounds of the total, meaning that effectively my car has launched 25 pounds of CO_2 into the atmosphere, where scientists say it will linger for hundreds or even thousands of years, helping to trap solar heat and turn the atmosphere into a greenhouse.

Richard Conniff, "Counting Carbons," *Discover,* August 2005, p. 57.

through the Book of Revelation.'"[14] Some prominent scientists doubt such a doomsday scenario. Patrick Michaels, a University of Virginia climate scientist and senior fellow of the Cato Institute, argues that increasing levels of carbon dioxide in the environment may actually be beneficial. He makes the case that since plants need carbon dioxide to grow, increased carbon dioxide levels actually enhance the production of food crops. He argues that good news like this is suppressed because "perhaps . . . there's little incentive for scientists to do anything but emphasize the negative and the destructive. Alarming news often leads to government funding, funding generates research, and research is the key to scientists' professional advancement."[15]

IS GLOBAL WARMING A PROBLEM?

"But what if the world is getting warmer? We don't really want to move into a new ice age, do we? If the earth is warming, why don't we all just put on some sunglasses and head to the beach? What's the problem?"

—Jerome R. Corsi and Craig R. Smith

Jerome R. Corsi and Craig R. Smith, *Black Gold Stranglehold*, Nashville, TN: WND Books, 2005, p. 94.

America's Dependence on Foreign Oil

Although some disagreement exists on the potential impact of global warming, there is little argument that America's appetite for oil has serious consequences. The foremost concern to most people—politicians and the general public alike—is that America cannot produce enough oil to fuel its own energy needs. In fact, the United States produces only about half the oil it consumes. As a result, the United States is dependent on purchasing oil from other countries. America imports 11 percent of its oil from Nigeria, 13 percent from Venezuela, and 25 percent from the Middle East. These regions are home to ongoing political conflicts and governments that do not always share the views of the United States.

"Oil addiction is America's Achilles' heel," explains author Matthew Yeomans. "To remain dominant in the world, the U.S. must be sure that oil flows freely and consistently onto the global market,"[16] he says. Robert E. Ebel of the Center for Strategic and International Studies agrees. "Oil fuels more than automobiles and airplanes. Oil fuels military power, national treasuries, and international politics."[17]

As early as 1980 securing America's access to Middle Eastern oil was a top concern for U.S. politicians. In his State of the Union speech, President Jimmy Carter stated: "Let our position be absolutely clear. An attempt by any outside force to gain control of the Persian Gulf region will be regarded as an assault on the vital interests of the United States of America and such an assault will be repelled by any means necessary, including military force."[18]

President George W. Bush has raised concerns over America's dependence on imported oil. To try and remedy the situation, he developed an energy initiative replacing 75 percent of oil imports from the Middle East by 2025.

Since that time, America has increased its military presence in the region as well as in the oil-producing countries of South America, Asia, and Africa. Author Michael T. Klare examines this trend in his book *Blood and Oil*. "Taken together, these developments lead to an inescapable conclusion: that the American military is being used more and more for the protection of overseas oil fields and the supply routes that connect them to the United States and its allies. . . . Slowly but surely, the U.S. military is being converted into a global oil-protection service."[19]

In a 2001 speech President George W. Bush voiced his concern about America's dependence on imported oil. "If we fail to act our country will become more reliant on foreign crude oil, putting our national energy security into the hands of foreign nations, some of whom do not share our interests."[20] To remedy the situation, the president developed an Advanced Energy Initiative with a goal of replacing 75 percent of oil imports from the Middle East by 2025. A future based on alternative energy may be possible, Bush says. "By applying the talent and technology of America, this country can dramatically improve our environment, move beyond a petroleum-based economy, and make our dependence on Middle Eastern oil a thing of the past."[21]

CHAPTER 2

DEVELOPING ALTERNATIVE VEHICLE FUELS

One important element in moving past a petroleum-based economy will be to find other means to power the vehicles that keep people and products moving. Currently transportation accounts for 30 percent of the world's energy use and 95 percent of global oil consumption. Over 700 million cars are on the road worldwide. With rising rates of car ownership, especially in developing regions of Asia, this number is expected to increase to over 1 billion by 2025.

America's Car Culture

The United States is currently the world's leader in car ownership and use. Americans drive 235 million cars, traveling over 7 billion miles each day. Although the United States' population has increased by only 40 percent since 1970, in that same period the number of miles Americans drive has increased 150 percent. As more and more people move from cities to suburbs and rural areas, they must spend more time in the car commuting to work or doing errands. On average, each day each American spends one hour in the car, and the average family generates about ten trips in their vehicles daily. These long and frequent trips add up; passenger vehicles in the United States consume 8.2 billion barrels of oil daily.

Despite rising gasoline prices, fears of dependence on foreign sources of oil, and a growing awareness of the environmental harm that cars cause, American consumers have so far proven unable to make significant changes in their driving habits. Cars afford a lifestyle of easy mobility and convenience that Americans have grown to depend on. Options that would reduce Americans' dependence on cars, such as comprehensive public transportation systems, have not been well developed. Clearly, cars are here to stay. "The bottom line is we can't change America's love affair with the automobile, but we can change the automobile,"[22] says Dan Becker of the Sierra Club, a conservation group that promotes alternative vehicles.

Electric Cars

Using alternative power sources for vehicles is not a totally new idea. In the 1970s as pollution increased and gasoline shortages began, the electric car was introduced as the first alternative to gasoline- or diesel-powered cars. Electric cars use no gasoline or diesel fuel. Instead, they use electric motors powered by current

The owner of a General Motors EV1 electric car plugs the charging cable in at a power station in 2001. A 2006 film, Who Killed the Electric Car?, *documented the rise and fall of the EV1.*

The prototype for the Mitsubishi Innovative Electric Vehicle, seen here in 2006, combines gasoline and electric power.

from onboard batteries. Once considered the most promising new vehicle technology, the electric car lost most of its early appeal because of its limited range. The electric car's weakness is its batteries. The batteries can provide enough electricity to power an electric car's travel for a maximum of only 100 miles (161km), after which time they must be plugged in for up to eight hours to recharge. This short range prevents the electric car from being a practical alternative for most American drivers, who regularly make longer trips.

Despite the downside of its limited range, the electric car does have significant benefits. An electric car costs less to maintain and lasts longer than a conventional car since it has fewer moving parts to wear out. The electricity cost of charging the car is lower than the gasoline costs for a conventional car. Perhaps most importantly, since it burns no oil, an electric car creates no pollution when running. However, for an accurate picture of the car's environmental impact, the pollution generated by the power plant providing the electricity for charging the batteries must be taken into account. The California Air Resources Board has studied electric cars and concluded that even when factoring in pollution from power plants, electric vehicles reduce pollution by over 90 percent compared to the newest and cleanest conventional vehicles.

The first commercial electric car was the EV1, developed by General Motors in 1996. However, the car was slow to catch on. People were apprehensive about having to plug in the cars, and some were unhappy with the car's performance. Eventually General Motors discontinued the EV1. This decision angered many electric car proponents. Chris Paine, one of the first EV1 owners, went on to direct a 2006 film, *Who Killed the Electric Car?*, documenting the rise and fall of the groundbreaking vehicle. "There are maybe 1,000 electric cars still on the road in California. It should have been a million,"[23] he says.

No Need for Oil Wars

"There is really no need going around starting wars over oil. We have it here at home. We have the necessary product, the farmers can grow it."

—Willie Nelson, founder of Willie Nelson's Biodiesel (a company that makes biodiesel fuel known as "BioWillie")

Quoted in Matt Curry, "Willie Nelson's New Gig: Biodiesel," MSNBC.com, January 14, 2005. www.msnbc.msn.com/id/6826994/.

Despite such setbacks, supporters of electric cars refuse to give up. New battery technology promises to improve the range of electric cars, overcoming the major stumbling block to developing broad appeal to consumers. New electric car entrepreneurs are trying to help the cars overcome their wimpy image as glorified golf carts. Martin Eberhard, founder of Tesla Motors, explains his company's philosophy. "Most electric cars were designed by and for people who fundamentally don't think we should drive. We at Tesla Motors love cars."[24] With a greater range, faster speed, and sexier image than previous electric cars, the one-hundred-thousand-dollar Tesla Roadster sports car represents a new direction for the electric car industry.

Hybrid Cars

Because current technology limits the potential to produce affordable electric cars that will have broad public appeal, most car manufacturers are looking at other alternatives. Much research focuses on boosting the fuel efficiency of cars—finding ways to drive longer distances using less gas. According to the Natural Resources Defense Council, raising the fuel efficiency of cars from the 2005 average of 24 miles per gallon (10km/l) to 40 miles per gallon (17km/l) would cut gasoline use in the United States by one-third and significantly reduce pollution.

Car manufacturers have been able to realize this level of fuel efficiency through the development of the hybrid car. The hybrid car is essentially a cross between a gasoline- or diesel-powered car and an electric car, combining the best features of

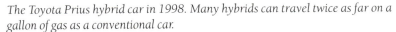

The Toyota Prius hybrid car in 1998. Many hybrids can travel twice as far on a gallon of gas as a conventional car.

both types of vehicles. Hybrid cars run on both a gasoline or diesel engine and an electric motor powered by batteries. The batteries in a hybrid car never need to be plugged in. Instead, the gas engine runs a generator that keeps the batteries charged. Because the electric motor helps to power the car, the gas engine of a hybrid is smaller than that of conventional cars and requires less fuel. The hybrid is controlled by a computer that automatically coordinates the operation of the engine and electric motor. At low speeds, the hybrid operates on the electric engine alone. Once a higher speed is reached, the gas engine takes over. Because the hybrid is under automatic control, drivers notice little difference from a conventional car.

CHEAP AND PLENTIFUL BIOFUELS

"Our mission is to make a gas that is so cheap and plentiful that consumers don't even have to know it's not made from fossil fuels."

—Martin Tobias, investor in Seattle Biodiesel

Quoted in *Newsweek*, "Ten Eco-Friendly Companies," November 21, 2005. www.msnbc.msn.com/id/10020271/site/newsweek/.

The hybrid's use of an electric motor to boost power allows it to realize significant fuel savings. Many hybrids can travel twice as far on a gallon of gas as a conventional car. The Toyota Prius, for example, averages 45 miles per gallon (19km/l), and the Honda Insight averages 60 miles per gallon (25km/l). Because they use less gas, hybrids also create less pollution.

Since the introduction of the first commercially available hybrid car in the United States in 1999, sales have doubled every year, supported in part by tax incentives available to those who purchase hybrids. Experts predict that by 2011 as many as thirty eight different hybrid models, including SUVs, pickup trucks, and sports cars, will be in automobile showrooms. The increasing popularity of hybrids has the potential eventually to make a significant impact on the amount of oil used to run vehicles in the United States. However, many new hybrid models use the electric motor to boost the cars' acceleration instead of dramatically

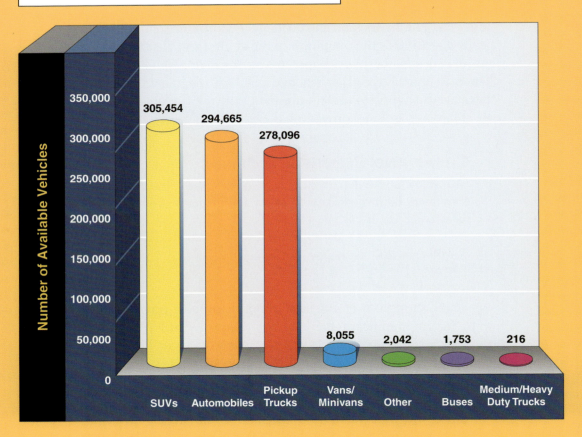

Availability of Alternative Fuel and Hybrid Vehicles in the U.S., 2005

Number of Available Vehicles

350,000

300,000

250,000

200,000

150,000

100,000

50,000

0

305,454 — SUVs

294,665 — Automobiles

278,096 — Pickup Trucks

8,055 — Vans/Minivans

2,042 — Other

1,753 — Buses

216 — Medium/Heavy Duty Trucks

Source: Energy Information Administration, Official Energy Statistics from the U.S. Government, www.eia.doe.gov/cneaf/alternate/page/datatables/atf14-20_05.html.

increasing the vehicle's gas mileage as achieved by the Prius and Insight. Critics argue that this application of hybrid technology defeats the purpose of saving gasoline and creates a false sense of energy conservation for the buyer. Most experts also caution that because they still require gas to operate, hybrids are only a temporary solution to declining oil supplies.

Biofuels

Although hybrid cars are currently the most widely available and popular approach to curbing the use of oil for powering vehicles, other solutions are quickly gaining prominence. One of the most promising is the use of biofuels, or fuels made from plants. Plants capture the energy of the sun through photosynthesis and store this energy in their tissues, such as their leaves, stems, and wood. When plants are used for fuel, they release the stored energy in the same way as fossil fuels. However, to make biofuels, plants are not just burned to create energy. Instead, biofuels are made by using a chemical process to transform the energy in plant tissues into a liquid fuel that can be used much like gasoline or diesel fuel.

There are two main types of biofuels: biodiesel and ethanol. Biodiesel is made from the vegetable oil found in plants such as

A woman fills up her truck with biodiesel fuel. Biodiesel fuel can be made from cooking oil recycled from restaurants, and vegetable oil found in plants such as soybeans and peanuts.

soybeans and peanuts. It can also be made from animal fats, including cooking oil recycled from restaurants. Biodiesel mixed with regular diesel fuel in the proportion of 20 percent biodiesel to 80 percent diesel (known as B20) can usually be used in any standard diesel engine. The pure form of biodiesel (known as B100, or 100 percent biodiesel) can be used in diesel engines with special modifications.

Instead of being made from oil-rich plants, ethanol is made from plants high in sugar, such as corn, sugar cane, and sugar beets. Through the process of fermentation, the sugar in the plants is transformed into ethanol, a type of alcohol. Ethanol is mixed with unleaded gasoline, usually in a mixture of 85 percent ethanol and 15 percent gasoline called E85. Vehicles that run on E85 are called flexible fuel, or flex-fuel, vehicles. (Flex-fuel vehicles can also run on unleaded gasoline.) An estimated 5 million flex-fuel vehicles are already on the road in the United States, although many of their owners are unaware they can run on E85 because, until recently, auto makers have not widely promoted this feature.

Both ethanol and biodiesel can be transported and sold in a similar manner as standard vehicle fuel. "Biofuels are the easiest fuels to slot into the existing fuel system,"[25] says Michael Pacheco, director of the National Bioenergy Center. Using biofuels creates much less pollution than standard fuels. When burned in cars, biofuels produce significantly less carbon dioxide and pollutants that contribute to smog and acid rain. Biofuels are nontoxic and will break down easily in the environment if they are spilled. Perhaps most importantly, biofuels are made up of mostly renewable plant resources. In their pure forms, biofuels will be available even when fossil fuels are used up.

Barriers to Biofuels

On the surface, biofuels seem like an easy solution to the problem of declining oil supplies. However, some significant challenges have so far prevented the widespread use of biofuels in the United States. In most places, the cost of both biodiesel and ethanol is higher than that of gasoline and diesel fuel. Until gas prices rise higher than those of biofuels or biofuel prices fall,

"The Saudi Arabia of Ethanol"

Because Brazil's climate provides the perfect year-round growing conditions for sugar-rich sugarcane, the country is able to cultivate large amounts of raw material for ethanol production. Decades of far-sighted planning have perfectly positioned Brazil as the world's leader in developing a network for producing, distributing, and even exporting this new international commodity. Stefan Theil of *Newsweek International* explains:

> The country's sugar-cane fields now feed a network of 320 ethanol plants, with 50 more planned in the next five years. Most of Brazil's 20 million drivers still tank up with fuel that is cut with 25 percent ethanol, but a growing fleet of new-generation (flex-fuel) cars can run on straight ethanol, which goes for as little as half the cost of gas at every service station from downtown Rio to the remote Amazon outback. To keep up with demand, local sugar barons and giant multinationals will invest some $6 million in new plantations and distilleries over the next five years. And Brazilian ethanol tankers are plying the seven seas, supplying fuel-hungry countries like South Korea and Japan as they begin to diversify away from oil. No wonder there's talk of Brazil's fast becoming "the Saudi Arabia of ethanol."

Stefan Theil, "The Next Petroleum," *Newsweek International,* August 8, 2005. www.msnbc.msn.com/id/87 69619/site/newsweek/.

Sugarcane fields surround ethanol storage tanks in Brazil, where eight out of every ten new cars run on ethanol.

consumers will be unlikely to be willing to pay more at the pump. Those willing to buy biofuels also face the challenge of finding filling stations that carry those fuels. In 2005, for example, there were only six hundred E85 fueling stations in thirty states, although many more are currently being installed.

The growth of the biofuel industry will also be determined by the amount of cropland available to grow the plants needed to make biofuels. One estimate shows that for the United States to replace 10 percent of the fuel used in transportation would require 40 percent of the nation's farmland. Using this much cropland could decrease the amount of available food and drive up food prices. It is thought that worldwide, there is not enough farmland to grow sufficient crops to manufacture enough biofuels to replace fossil fuels totally.

Some experts also debate the real fuel-saving impact that biofuels have. Growing and harvesting the crops, powering the factories that turn the plants into fuel, and transporting the fuel require large amounts of energy, usually from fossil fuels. Estimates of the actual amount of energy gained by making biofuels range widely. One study showed that it takes two-thirds of a gallon (2.5l) of oil to make 1 gallon (3.8l) of ethanol from corn. Therefore, using a gallon of ethanol would save only one-third of a gallon (1.25l) of gas. "There are many in the energy community who believe that the amount in the oil that you use to produce a gallon of ethanol is about the same as you get out of it once you've made it,"[26] says Ryan Wiser, a scientist at Lawrence Berkeley National Laboratory.

The Future of Biofuels

Those statistics could change as a result of research underway into a new form of ethanol production. Faced with the challenge of producing more fuel without using more farmland, researchers have discovered a way to utilize more than just the sugar-rich parts of plants to make ethanol. Called cellulosic ethanol, this fuel is made from the cellulose that comprises the structural parts of plants, such as their stems, bark, and leaves. This new process will allow many more types of plants to be used for making biofuels, including plants such as poplar trees and grasses that grow to a large size very quickly and agricultural waste such as cornstalks. As a result, more biofuels will be produced per acre of land, reducing both the cost of production and energy use.

These new developments in the biofuel industry have generated excitement among investors who hope to bring large amounts of the fuel at lower prices to the commercial market. Both the oil company BP and agriculture giant Cargill plan to invest huge sums to finance biofuel research and production. Greg Stephanopolous, a chemical engineering professor at Massachusetts Institute of Technology, predicts it will take ten years and hundreds of millions of dollars to bring cellulosic ethanol to market. "That's the downside," he says. "The upside is the potential to replace tens of billions of dollars in oil imports. It's a no-brainer."[27]

Although the United States is now vigorously pursuing biofuel research, it lags behind other countries that already have strong biofuel programs. Most notable is Brazil, where the

President George W. Bush discusses the applications of cellulosic ethanol with Thomas Nagy, president and plant manager for the biotech company Novozymes North America, in 2007.

development of an ethanol industry started in 1975. Today Brazil produces 3.5 billion gallons (13.2 billion l) of ethanol a year, accounting for half of all the vehicle fuel in the country. Biodiesel is already a popular fuel in Europe, where over 600 million gallons (2.2 billion l) are produced annually. Thailand, China, South Africa, and Australia are also making large investments in biofuel production.

GREEN IS NOW MAINSTREAM

"The green, sustainability movement is going mainstream and we want to ride that wave."

—AOL founder Steve Case, who has invested in alternative vehicle projects

Quoted in Annys Shin, "Internet Visionaries Betting on Green Technology Boom," *Washington Post,* April 18, 2006, p. D1.

Harnessing Hydrogen as a Vehicle Fuel

Biofuels are not the only alternative vehicle fuel technology generating corporate and government interest and research funding. Another potential fuel source has recently been emerging from the realms of science fiction to a position where many believe it is poised to transform the world's energy system. This fuel source is hydrogen.

Hydrogen is the most abundant element in the universe. On earth, however, it rarely exists in its free state. Instead, it binds to other elements such as oxygen and carbon to form water, plant material, and fossil fuels. Instead of being an energy source itself, such as oil or coal, hydrogen is an energy carrier in the same manner as electricity. In other words, in order to provide energy, hydrogen must first be produced by using an energy source to free it from its bonds with other elements.

Hydrogen powers a car by creating electricity within a special onboard device called a fuel cell. A chemical reaction takes place as hydrogen enters the fuel cell, splitting the electrons off the hydrogen molecules to produce electricity that powers the car's motor. Fuel cell–powered cars produce no pollution or greenhouse gases; only a small amount of water emerges from the tailpipe as a result of the chemical reaction.

Is Hydrogen a Viable Solution?

Hydrogen may seem like an environmentalist's dream solution to the problems of fossil fuels. However, developing hydrogen as a widespread vehicle fuel has many stumbling blocks that must be resolved before this dream can become reality. Perhaps the most significant challenge lies with the production of the hydrogen itself. Currently the raw materials used to produce hydrogen are primarily natural gas and coal. Extracting hydrogen from these materials requires a great deal of energy and releases carbon. In fact, the amount of energy required to produce the hydrogen is about the same as the amount of energy the hydrogen produces to propel a car. So although a hydrogen-powered car may produce no pollution itself, the entire process still requires fossil fuels and creates harmful emissions.

To solve these problems, researchers are focusing on ways to produce hydrogen from water through a process called electrolysis. Although it eliminates the need for fossil fuels for raw material, electrolysis is a complex and expensive process that also requires a great deal of energy. Other research is focused on using renewable energy sources such as solar or wind power to

Systems engineer Jeffrey Schmidt stands next to his hydrogen-fueled car protoype in 2006. Hydrogen fuelcell powered cars produce no pollution or greenhouse gases.

provide the energy needed to generate hydrogen from water. Princeton professor Kenneth Deffeyes believes that goal is within reach. "There is no absolute scientific barrier to using renewable wind- or solar-generated electricity to produce hydrogen from water,"[28] he says. If that goal is achieved, hydrogen fuel cell cars will truly be pollution free.

Producing hydrogen is only the first step. To be an effective vehicle fuel, it must be easy for consumers to purchase and store in their cars. Hydrogen is most commonly used in its gas form. However, hydrogen gas takes up a great deal more space than its energy equivalent in gasoline. This makes it difficult to store a large amount in the small space of a car's gas tank. To overcome this obstacle, hydrogen gas can be compressed and stored in strong, high-pressure tanks. However, these tanks pose a risk of explosion if punctured. Hydrogen can also be stored as a liquid but needs to be cooled to -423°F (-253°C). Because hydrogen is highly flammable, further research is required to develop a storage system that will be both safe and cost-effective.

NO END TO THE OIL AGE

"The Stone Age did not end because we ran out of stones, and the oil age will not end because we run out of oil."
—Don Huberts, CEO of Shell Hydrogen

Quoted in Christine Woodside, *The Homeowner's Guide to Energy Independence.* Guilford, CT: Lyons, 2006, p. 64.

Despite the challenges, many alternative energy experts have expressed the view that hydrogen will play a large role in the future of global energy use. President George W. Bush has dedicated over a billion dollars of government funding for hydrogen innovation. Hydrogen fuel cells have powered city buses (with space to handle large hydrogen storage containers) in several pilot programs around the world since 2002. Iceland is producing hydrogen using nonpolluting hydroelectric and geothermal power; Shell has already opened a hydrogen filling station in that country.

Although some progress is slowly being made, the question remains as to whether or not the use of hydrogen can ramp up

Oil from Anything?

Another new source of fuel may be as close as the garbage can. Through a process called thermal conversion, almost any organic material can be transformed into oil. The first commercial thermal conversion plant was built in Missouri next to a turkey processing plant. Waste from the turkey slaughterhouse is processed in a manner that replicates what happened to the remains of ancient animals during the formation of fossil fuels. The waste under-goes a treatment of high pressure and temperature that breaks down the chains of hydrogen and carbon molecules, transforming the raw material into oil and some by-products. The oil is separated and sold as fuel to power generators at electric plants. It can also be further refined into diesel fuel, gasoline, or hydrogen. This process is highly efficient; 85 percent of the energy of the raw materials remains in the final product.

quickly enough to solve the world's looming energy crisis. Experts estimate that fuel cell cars will not be on the consumer market until at least 2020. This is in part because hydrogen providers are not likely to build hydrogen-fueling stations unless there are enough fuel cell vehicles on the road. But automakers are not likely to build fuel cell vehicles unless a network of hydrogen fueling stations exists.

Perhaps the best indicator that a transition to hydrogen may be underway is the fact that many oil companies and automakers have committed billions of dollars to this developing technology. Energy experts predict that if a move is made to a hydrogen economy, it will be as significant a chapter in the energy history of the world as the discovery of fossil fuels.

Seth Dunn of WorldWatch Institute states the need for urgency. "Countries that focus their efforts on producing oil until the resource is gone will be left behind in the rush for tomorrow's prize,"[29] he says. Whether the ultimate "prize" will be hydrogen fuel cells, biofuels, or hybrid-electric cars remains to be seen. Don Huberts, former director of Shell's hydrogen division, observes the uncertainty of the outcome. "Everyone is placing bets on several horses. By no means is it clear today which the winner will be."[30]

WHAT IS THE POTENTIAL OF SOLAR POWER?

One strong contender in the race for a source of abundant and clean energy is solar power. The idea of harnessing the power of the sun for widespread use as an energy source first emerged during the energy crisis of the 1970s. President Jimmy Carter proposed the increased use of solar power to replace up to 20 percent of the United States' fossil fuel needs by 2000. However, once oil shortages eased and gas prices dropped, attitudes toward solar power shifted. Most Americans considered solar power to be an awkward technology best suited for radical environmentalists. As a result, solar power never really caught on.

GREAT ELECTRICITY MARKET

"The electricity market is as big as the sky."
—Erik Straser of Mohr Davidow Ventures, a firm investing in emerging solar companies

Quoted in Charles Piller, "Pioneering Technology Lab Now Puts Energy into Solar," *Los Angeles Times,* July 3, 2006, p. C1.

However, as oil prices rise again and fears of depleting oil supplies loom, solar power is getting another look. There are good reasons to look to the sun for energy. The sun provides, by far, the largest source of renewable energy known. More energy from sunlight reaches the earth in one hour than the total amount of energy the earth consumes in one entire year. Using solar power creates no pollution or global warming emissions.

Despite its benefits, however, solar energy currently provides less than 0.1 percent of the world's electricity needs. The primary limitation of solar power is finding ways to turn sunlight into an energy form that can be widely used.

Some researchers never abandoned their faith in the potential of solar power and have continued to pursue new methods to make it a feasible alternative to traditional energy sources. As a result of the progress made in developing new solar technologies, many energy experts believe that the power of the sun holds huge promise for supplementing or even replacing fossil fuel use worldwide.

Solar Power Systems

There are currently three ways to use the energy from the sun: passive solar systems, solar thermal systems, and photovoltaic cells. Passive systems rely on building techniques and materials to save energy from the sun without using any mechanical means. Examples of passive solar energy use include greenhouses and homes designed with windows facing south to gain maximum advantage of the sun's rays. Because buildings consume a great deal

Greenhouses are examples of passive solar energy.

of energy for heating and cooling, these methods are valuable for improving a building's energy efficiency and reducing its fossil fuel needs. However, passive solar systems cannot transform the sun's energy into other useful forms.

Instead of simply saving the sun's energy, thermal solar systems use mechanical methods to collect, control, and store the flow of energy from sunlight. The most basic thermal systems consist of panels mounted on a building's roof. Sunlight heats water or other fluid running through pipes within the panels. This hot water is then pumped through a device called a heat exchanger that transfers the heat from the pipes to water in a storage tank. The heated water can be used for bathing or to warm a building's floor through radiant heating.

Because they are relatively easy and affordable to install, home solar hot water systems are in wide use around the world. Since water heaters make up to 25 percent of the energy used by a home, a widespread shift to solar water heating systems has the potential to reap significant money and energy savings. Several countries, including Israel and Spain, now require solar water heaters to be installed in all new buildings. However, small-scale solar thermal systems provide only very localized and limited benefits from the sun's energy. That is, the heat in the water cannot be transported far from where it is gathered, and it cannot be used as energy to provide power for other uses.

Solar Power Plants

Instead of simply transporting the sun's heat, larger, more complex solar thermal systems are used to convert solar energy into electricity. These systems operate in a manner similar to that of traditional power plants to produce electricity that can be transmitted to multiple homes and businesses. Just as in a traditional power plant, an industrial solar thermal system heats water to create steam that is used to turn turbines, generating electricity. With a solar plant, however, water is heated through the sun's energy instead of by burning coal or natural gas.

Solar thermal plants, also known as concentrating solar power systems, are designed to capture as much energy from the sun as possible. They are usually located in places that

Solar thermal plants, also known as concentrating solar power systems, are designed to capture as much energy from the sun as possible.

receive the most sunlight. In the United States, plants have been installed in the deserts of California, Nevada, and New Mexico. To capture sunlight, these plants employ hundreds of large, curved mirrors, called heliostats, specially programmed to rotate to track the movement of the sun. The mirrors reflect the sunlight in a concentrated beam aimed at a central tower. The intense heat that results boils water in the tower's tank, creating steam that drives the electricity-producing turbines.

The first large solar power plant was an experimental facility called Solar One, built in California's Mojave Desert in 1981. After operating successfully for four years, Solar One was converted to Solar Two, which used molten salt instead of water to capture heat. Salt proved better at storing the sun's energy, allowing the system to continue generating heat to operate during times of cloud cover and after nightfall. The plant produced enough power to supply ten thousand homes until the experiment ended and Solar Two was closed in 1999.

Solar Power from Space

One proposed application of solar power seems more suited to science fiction than real life. Space solar power, or SSP, would capture sunlight using huge photovoltaic arrays orbiting the earth. The energy generated would be converted to microwaves and sent down to earth, where the microwaves would be captured by an antenna and transformed into usable electricity.

NASA first studied the concept of space solar power during the energy crisis of the 1970s, but technology did not support the idea at the time. In 1995 in light of advances in photovoltaic technology, NASA took another look at getting energy from space. NASA determined that within several decades, it would be possible to have a system in place that could generate small amounts of electricity. With continued advances in technology, the agency predicts that by 2050, large-scale energy transmission to earth could take place. Dr. Neville Marzwell, a technical manager for NASA, is optimistic about the future of SSP. "With funding and support, we can continue developing this technology," he says. "We offer an advantage. You don't need cables, pipes, gas, or copper wires. We can send it to you like a cell phone call—where you want it and when you want it, in real time."

Quoted in Science@NASA, "Beam It Down, Scotty!" March 23, 2001. http://science.nasa.gov/headlines/y2001/ast23mar_1.htm.

The Stirling Engine

While Solar One and Solar Two proved that solar plants could provide power for large communities, their downside was that they produced far less power than traditional power plants. By the time it is captured and used to create electricity in this process, only about 10 to 15 percent of the sunlight's energy is actually converted into power. To increase the efficiency of solar plants, engineers are experimenting with an engine invented nearly two hundred years ago.

Called the Stirling engine, this machine is powered by hydrogen gas contained within an internal chamber. The gas expands when heated and compresses when cooled, creating a force that moves a piston inside the engine to generate electricity. Unlike internal combustion engines (such as those used in cars or factories), the Stirling engine is a closed system that burns no fuel. Therefore, it creates no exhaust and no pollution. Creating electricity with the Stirling engine is twice as efficient as heating water to generate steam. Almost 30 percent of captured sunlight is converted into electrical energy using this method.

The hydrogen in each Stirling engine is heated by its own giant array of mirrors, called a concentrator. Each 38-foot-diameter concentrator (11.6m) is made up of ninety sun-tracking mirrors, each the size and shape of an automobile hood. The concentrator is aimed at the oil-barrel-sized engine suspended in front. Each array provides enough heat for the engine to power a 25-kilowatt generator.

Stirling Energy, the company that produces the Stirling engine, is putting its technology to the test with the construction of an enormous 4,500-acre solar energy farm (1,821ha) in the Mojave Desert. Starting with forty mirror-and-engine arrays by the end of 2006, the company plans to expand into a plant able to generate 500 megawatts of power using twenty thousand arrays by 2012. That would be enough electricity to power a quarter of a million Southern California homes.

SOLAR CELLS ARE A GREAT ENERGY SOURCE

"Solar cells are truly a dream power source. They are silent, highly reliable, portable, convenient, risk-free, pollution-free, recyclable, technologically elegant, suitable for utility or customer use, mass producible, long-lived, and thoroughly compatible with a sustainable economy."

—John J. Berger

John J. Berger, *Charging Ahead*. New York: Holt, 1997, p. 53.

Although they are the most efficient solar generators around, Stirling Energy's huge solar arrays and engines are not likely to become available to the masses. Besides their large size, they are extremely expensive—about $250,000 each. When mass-produced as the company plans, however, the cost of each unit is expected to drop enough to make the power profitable. The company sees the potential of this system to help power companies in California meet the government's requirement that 20 percent of electricity they sell must be from renewable sources by 2017. In fact, a solar energy plant covering a total area of 100 square miles (256 sq. km) could, in theory, generate enough renewable, nonpolluting electricity to supply the entire United States.

Photovoltaic Cells

While breakthroughs in solar thermal technology may eventually prove valuable in advancing the use of solar power, another method for creating electricity from sunlight is now attracting a great deal of attention. This method is the use of photovoltaic cells. Also known as solar cells, photovoltaic cells generate electricity directly from sunlight through an electronic process inside. Most people are already familiar with the solar cells that power calculators and satellites in orbit, but advancements in photovoltaic technology may soon allow solar power to be more widely applied for providing energy to homes and businesses.

Photovoltaic cells are made from electricity-conducting materials called semiconductors—the same materials used to make computer chips. The most commonly used semiconduc-

The headquarters of Solarex, a maker of solar energy products, has a solar panel array attached to the main building to generate electrical power.

tor is the element silicon. When light hits the photovoltaic cell, the silicon inside absorbs a portion of its energy. This transfer of energy knocks off some of the silicon atom's electrons, allowing them to flow freely and creating electric current. This current can either be used directly or stored in batteries for later use.

Solar cells have been used to make electricity since the 1950s. Early photovoltaic technology relied on large, bulky collectors that converted only 10 to 15 percent of the sun's energy to power. New systems, however, are much more sophisticated and concentrate the sunlight as much as five hundred times better. As a result, these solar cells currently capture as much as 30 percent of the sun's energy and are projected to improve efficiency up to 50 percent in the near future.

Increasing the efficiency of photovoltaic cells will result in lower costs for solar power systems. Because electricity purchased from power companies is relatively inexpensive, the cost of solar power must be low enough to compete before most consumers will make the transition. The U.S. Department of Energy believes that the cost of solar power will be about equal to that of electricity generated by fossil fuels by about 2015, but new technology may advance that estimate.

Despite its cost, solar power using photovoltaic cells is already catching on. Small, inexpensive systems are in widespread use powering outdoor lighting, railroad crossing signals, agricultural water pumps, and electric fencing. Homeowners are also beginning to use photovoltaic cells for their electricity needs. Although there are up-front costs of installing the solar cells on the home's roof, there are also many incentives offered by the government to encourage the use of solar power. Tax credits, rebates, and grants help homeowners in some states pay off the cost of a system in a relatively short period of time. For example, one homeowner in Southern California spent twenty-one thousand dollars on a photovoltaic system and other energy saving upgrades, but paid only nine thousand dollars himself after incentives. He will also receive a tax credit of two thousand dollars each year for several years.

The benefits of a home or business solar power system are considerable. Not only does the home consume significantly

Spreading the Light

Canadian electrical engineering professor Dr. Dave Irvine-Halliday is working to change the lives of rural villagers who have no electricity for lighting. While on a trek in Nepal, Irvine-Halliday visited a villager's hut and was amazed by the lack of light and thick smoke swirling from the cooking fire inside. Thoughts of the visit nagged him as he returned home, eventually inspiring him to develop a source of simple and economical light that could be used in those remote places.

After much experimentation, Irvine-Halliday developed a system that connected simple lights called diodes to batteries charged by solar panels. Each system will last for decades and costs about ninety dollars—a bargain compared to the seventy-dollar cost for a villager's year's supply of kerosene. When he returned to Nepal to test his system, it was so well received that he established the Light Up the World Foundation to bring light to the millions of people who live in darkness. Light Up the World is working with partners to bring down the cost of the system's components and provide grant funding so even the poorest villagers can benefit. Since Light Up the World was founded, over fourteen thousand homes in twenty-six countries have been wired for light. When he flips the switch on a newly wired system, it's an exciting moment. Says Irvine-Halliday: "I feel what the villagers feel, that they've got light, real light for the first time. It's almost indescribable."

Quoted in CNN.com, "Global Usage of Solar Power Grows," transcript of *Global Challenges* interview, International Wire, July 22, 2006. http://transcripts.cnn.com/TRANSCRIPTS/0607/22/gc.01.html.

less energy, the homeowner or business owner can actually sell excess power generated to the local utility company. Modern home photovoltaic systems are connected to the power grid that supplies electricity from a power plant. In times of extended cloudy weather or large power needs, the home can still receive power through the grid. However, when producing more power than the home consumes, the flow of electricity reverses, sending power back to the utility company. Federal law dictates that by 2008, all U.S. power companies must pay the homeowner or business owner for the power generated. More than half of all states already follow this practice. Tony Ellsworth, owner of a custom bike company, installed a rooftop photovoltaic system when he built his new factory. The benefits of this system have helped him cope with times of stress running his business. "I deal with the low moments by going out back and watching the electric meter run backward," he says. "That always puts a smile on my face."[31]

Solar Catches On

While the use of solar power may not yet have moved into the mainstream in the United States, worldwide use of solar power is growing quickly. The global solar industry has grown over 30 percent each year from 2001 to 2006. Germany is the leader in using solar power, accounting for 57 percent of all solar installations in 2005 (compared to just 7 percent for the United States). Other European countries and Japan are also looking to the sun to meet their future power needs. Currently Japan accounts for 20 percent of the solar market, but the Japanese

New, sophisticated photovoltaic cells are able to concentrate the sunlight as much as five hundred times better than older cells.

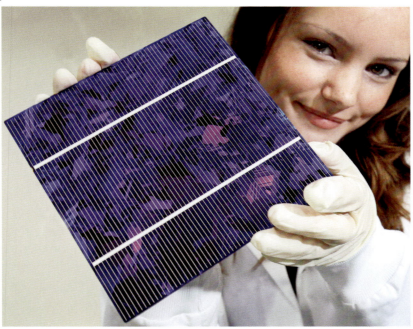

government expects that by 2030, 50 percent of the power used in homes in that country will be solar based.

Another developing market for solar energy is China. China still generates most of its power by burning coal. As a result, China has the worst air pollution in the world. Some large Chinese cities such as Beijing have banned the use of home coal boilers in an attempt to begin clearing the air. Solar power is quickly catching on as an alternative. It is becoming increasingly common to see solar panels on the roofs of the city's homes and factories.

Power to Change Lives

Outside of China's cities, many Chinese live in small, rural villages with little or no power available. Bringing large-scale solar power to China would not only improve air quality, it would improve the lives of millions of peasant farmers. Himin Solar Energy Group, founded in 1996, manufactures solar water heaters for Chinese families. With sales growing at 100 percent each year, Himin has already supplied solar water heaters to 40 million families throughout China. For the first time, millions of people can take hot baths and use warm water to wash clothes and dishes.

WE'RE DRILLING A HOLE IN THE SKY

"We are in effect drilling a hole into the sky, direct to the sun, getting fresh solar energy from up above. They're using fossilized solar energy from below."

—Newton Becker, solar power proponent

Quoted in John J. Berger, *Charging Ahead*. New York: Holt, 1997, p. 43.

In fact, perhaps solar power's most significant benefit is its potential for improving the lives of the estimated 2 billion people around the world who live without electricity for basic needs such as lighting, refrigeration, or pumping water. Connecting isolated and impoverished villages to existing power grids is nearly impossible in many countries.

In Nigeria, for example, less than 36 percent of the population has access to electricity. To connect each village to the national power grid would cost an estimated $1.2 million. Nigeria, with a tropical climate ideal for using solar power, is experimenting with establishing solar systems that would cost only about eighty-three thousand dollars per village. The first of nineteen villages to gain electricity in the government's pilot project is a small fishing community on a coastal island, reachable only by boat. The island's five thousand people have never before had electricity. Now village residents can light their main street, churches, and mosques, provide electricity for their elementary school, and feel better connected to the outside world. "The project has brought great joy and relief to us . . . we now have access to information more than before when we depended on battery-powered radio. We can now watch television and charge our mobile phones,"[32] explains one island resident.

Can the United States Go Solar?

People in remote places have been quick to embrace solar power because it brings such significant improvements to their lives. In places that already have a high standard of living, however, such as the United States, people have been slower to accept solar power as a viable source of energy. That attitude may soon change as both the federal and some state governments have begun to promote strongly the use of solar power.

California is the nation's leader in solar energy technology. In August 2006 California governor Arnold Schwarzenegger signed legislation to implement his Million Solar Roofs plan. The plan's goal is to install 1 million new solar systems on roofs in California by 2018. If accomplished, this initiative will produce 3,000 megawatts of electricity, or the equivalent of five electric power plants. It will also reduce greenhouse gas emissions by 3 million tons (2.72 billion kg)—the equivalent of taking 1 million cars off the road. Provisions of the plan include increasing incentives for going solar and requiring home builders to provide solar options to customers.

The federal government is also promoting solar power through President Bush's 2007 Solar America Initiative. This initiative provides nearly $150 million in research money to improve and reduce the cost of photovoltaic and concentrating

California governor Arnold Schwarzenegger signed legislation to implement his Million Solar Roofs plan in 2006, which calls for the installation of 1 million new solar systems on roofs in California by 2018.

solar power systems. This commitment to renewable energy from an administration known for its close ties to the oil industry may signal a shift in American attitude that energy experts hope will be long lasting. Ron Larson, chair of the American Solar Energy Society, has worked with the government on solar policy since the 1970s, "experiencing more than one policy 'mood swing' for renewable energy. This time I believe the mood swing is for real,"[33] he says. Larson and other proponents of renewable, clean solar power hold hope that it will ultimately emerge as one component of the solution to the world's energy challenge.

CHAPTER 4

Harnessing Energy from the Earth

In addition to advancing the use of solar power, many researchers are also examining the potential of more earthbound sources of clean and abundant energy for replacing fossil fuels. These sources include wind, the movement of ocean waves and tides, and heat from below the earth's surface. Some of these sources, such as the power of the sea, are only in the beginning, experimental stages of development as a viable means for producing power. Others, such as wind power and using the earth's heat, have already been put into fairly wide use in some parts of the world.

Wind Power Makes Sense

"Wind works. It's reliable. It's economical. It makes environmental sense. And it's here now. Wind machines are not tomorrow's technology."

—Paul Gipe

Paul Gipe, *Wind Power.* White River Junction, VT: Chelsea Green, 2004, p. 1.

Wind Power

One of the most common forms of alternative energy is wind power. In some respects, wind is actually a form of solar energy. As the sun shines down, it heats the atmosphere and the earth's surface. However, variation in land formations, vegetation, and bodies of water causes uneven heating around the planet. Air in some areas, such as at the equator, warms quickly. As this warm air expands and rises, cooler air rushes in to replace it. The warmed air eventually cools and sinks back to the earth. This movement of warm and cool air combined with the rotational force of the earth creates wind.

People have been harnessing energy from the wind for thousands of years. Long before the discovery of coal or oil, sailing vessels traveled the world powered only by the wind in their sails. Windmills used for pumping water and grinding grain have been a common sight in the countryside of Europe for centuries. In these cases, wind is put to direct work, pushing ships and powering wheels to move water and grind grain. The energy that results stays in the location where it is generated. More recent technology, however, has allowed the wind's energy to be used indirectly by converting it into electricity that can be transmitted long distances and used for many different purposes.

The inner workings of a wind turbine. The moving rotor spins a drive shaft connected to a generator that converts the energy from the wind's movement into electricity.

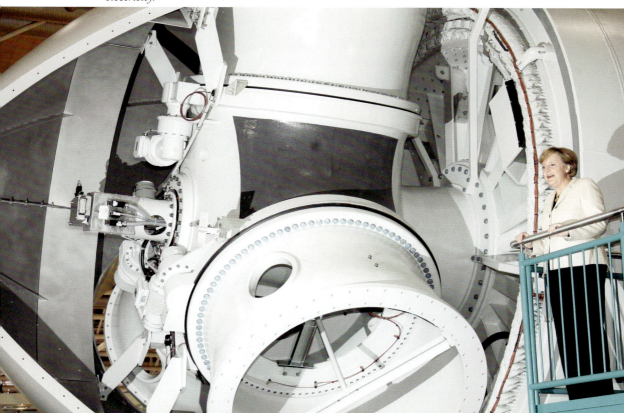

Farming the Wind

Wind technology has changed a great deal since the times of the classic Dutch windmills. Instead of employing wide, wooden sails mounted on broad, stout bases, energy from wind is now gathered by tall, sleek machines called turbines. The turbine is topped by a rotor made up of two or three long blades that spin in the wind. The moving rotor spins a drive shaft connected to a generator that converts the energy from the wind's movement into electricity. The electricity is sent through cables to a power substation from which it is distributed to distant cities.

Wind turbines are often built in clusters called wind farms. Proper placement of a wind farm is critical. Wind does not blow evenly in every location; some places are much more consistently windy than others. Additionally, wind speed changes throughout the day and from season to season. Wind farms need to be situated far from buildings and land features that can disrupt wind flow and create turbulence that can damage a turbine. All of these factors make it difficult to determine the best site for a wind farm. Wind scientists use complex mathematical calculations to account for these factors when selecting a site. Some of the best sites for wind farms are along coasts, lakeshores, and low-elevation ridgelines. New projects have even installed wind farms out at sea where strong winds consistently blow.

Wind scientists have also contributed a great deal to increasing the efficiency of generating power from the wind. Understanding the dynamics of wind allows for turbines that are better designed to catch more wind and convert it to electricity. Sophisticated computer controls constantly fine-tune the turbines, automatically adjusting the pitch of the blades to respond to changes in wind speed or direction. Turbines designed in the early 1980s generated an average power of only about 50 kilowatts. The largest modern turbines now, however, can each produce 1,800 kilowatts of electricity, enough to supply power to six hundred homes.

Wind turbines that generate that much power are very large. Commercial turbines already in widespread use have blades over 130 feet (40m) long, giving the rotor a diameter of over 260 feet (80m)—nearly the length of a football field. These turbines are mounted on towers 260 feet (80m) tall. Since wind blowing a few hundred feet above the ground may be up to five times stronger than that at the surface, these tall towers place the rotors in the best position for catching the most wind possible. One experimental turbine reaches 600 feet (183m) high and can generate an enormous 5 megawatts of power. Large wind farms may consist of hundreds, or even thousands, of turbines covering hundreds of acres of land. These large wind farms generate enough electricity to power an entire town.

Not all turbines are so big. Farms, small businesses, and homes also use wind turbines to provide power directly to their own electrical systems. These small systems use turbines with rotor diameters 50 feet (15m) or less, mounted on towers 120 feet (35m) tall or less. Home and farm turbines are often connected to batteries so the electricity generated can be stored for use when it is needed or when the wind does not blow.

Wind Power Around the World

Both small and large wind turbines are increasing in use all over the world. In fact, wind power is the world's fastest growing energy source. Europe leads the world in utilizing wind power. Denmark already uses wind power to supply 20 percent of its electricity. Germany, Spain, and England have also invested heavily in wind technology. A study performed by the European Wind Energy Association found that wind could provide 10 percent of the world's total electricity by 2017. That amount is the equivalent of powering the needs of 500 million European households.

North America uses only about one-fifth the amount of wind power that Europe does, but its wind industry is growing quickly. In the twenty-five years between 1981 and 2006, the amount of wind-generated electricity produced in the United States increased nine hundredfold. If the wind industry maintains its growth, by the year 2020, 6 percent of the nation's electricity could be generated by wind power. Most wind farms in the United States are in California, Texas, Minnesota, Iowa, and

The Ethics of Wind Farms

Peter Harper of the Center for Alternative Technology in Wales studies the environmental impacts of both fossil fuels and renewable energy alternatives. Harper agrees with critics of wind farms that say they contribute to a decline in the beauty of the landscape. However, he maintains that in sharp contrast to the use of fossil fuels, clean, safe, renewable wind energy should be embraced for ethical reasons.

Nearly all objectors to wind farms live in rural areas and don't want their landscapes spoiled. This is quite understandable; neither do I. But such people invariably wish to retain the benefits of abundant cheap energy, brought to them discreetly by means of cables, pipelines and tankers, for whom others (mostly in urban areas or overseas) have borne the impact of mining, refining, conversion, transmission etc, not to mention the wider implications of CO_2 [carbon dioxide] release. This is simply hypocritical. In opposing wind power on grounds of personal aesthetics, objectors are implicitly supporting something far worse, and trying to avoid paying their dues. . . . Now much as I hate the sight of these monsters in the countryside, they bring me some relief from my appalling hypocrisy. As I gaze upon them, it dawns on me that *I am now paying the environmental bill.* . . . So of all the sources I could choose, wind is one of the honest ones, where I can pick up the tab myself, right now. To oppose it on grounds of personal taste would be an act of the grossest and most shameful NIMBYism [slang term meaning "not in my backyard"].

Peter Harper, "Why I Hate Wind Farms and Think There Should Be More of Them," in *ReNew* No. 107, May/June 1997.

Wyoming. These five states produce two-thirds of the nation's wind-generated electricity. Forty-six states, however, have adequate winds to support the commercial use of wind power. Many of these states have projects in development.

One reason for the increased use of wind power is the falling cost of capturing the wind's energy. The cost of wind power has decreased to a level where it is now competitive with gas- and

A wind farm off the coast of the United Kingdom. Large wind farms may consist of hundreds, or even thousands, of turbines covering hundreds of acres of land or water.

coal-powered electrical plants. In addition, the payoffs of wind power are significant. Home systems in the windiest areas can save consumers up to 90 percent on their electric bills. Farmers and landowners can also generate significant income by leasing the wind rights of their land to power companies who establish wind farms there. Power companies also pay taxes to the communities where their wind farms are located. This revenue helps many economically challenged rural communities pay for much needed emergency services and equipment.

There are also significant environmental and social benefits to generating electricity from the wind instead of traditional power plants. Wind power creates no waste, pollution, or greenhouse gases. According to the American Wind Energy Association, a 1-megawatt turbine prevents 1,800 tons (1.63 million kg) of carbon dioxide from being released into the environment each year—the equivalent of planting 1 square mile

(2.56 sq. km) of forest. Unlike power plants that need water for cooling, wind farms have no need for water and can therefore be built in arid regions. Smaller wind turbines are cost-effective for bringing power to remote villages in the world's developing regions.

Challenges of Wind Power

Although getting energy from the wind has many benefits, there are also some drawbacks. The primary challenge in using the wind for energy is that the wind does not always blow. If there is no wind to turn the turbines, no electricity is generated. To solve this problem, most power companies use wind power as only one component of their overall energy strategy. Traditional power plants or solar power join wind power to form an integrated, hybrid energy system.

Another challenge with wind power is that, despite the fact that it does not contribute to the environmental damage associated with the use of fossil fuels, it does have some negative effects on the environment. Wildlife such as birds and bats are sometimes killed by the turbines' spinning rotors. This has been

Five hundred raptors have been killed at the wind farm at Altamont Pass in California since the facility began operation in the 1980s.

a significant problem at the Altamont Pass in California, east of San Francisco. This is the site of one of the largest and oldest wind farms in the United States, where 6,000 wind turbines generate enough power for 120,000 homes. The Altamont Pass is an important migration route for birds, especially raptors such as golden eagles and red-tailed hawks. Five hundred raptors have been killed since the facility began operation in the 1980s. Study of the problem has resulted in changes in tower structure to discourage perching, and other steps have also been taken to minimize the impact on wildlife. Most other wind farms, however, report very low rates of bird deaths—significantly less than those killed in collisions with buildings and vehicles.

NEED TO TRANSFORM OUR ENERGY SYSTEM

"It's a major psychological and cultural challenge for the environmental and conservation movement. What we need to combat climate change is a complete transformation of our energy system, and that requires a lot of new stuff to be built and installed, some of it in places that are relatively untouched."

—Stephen Tindale, executive director of Greenpeace UK

Quoted in Heather Timmons, "A Renewable Source, and Clean, but Not Without Its Critics," *New York Times*, August 3, 2006, p. C1.

A New Environmental Debate

Most debate about using wind power is not based on any actual environmental harm, but on how wind turbines impact their surroundings. Wind farms are very visible and often take up lots of space. Therefore, they dramatically change the landscape where they are built. Because areas of good wind are also often quite scenic, the installation of wind farms sometimes creates serious opposition from people in surrounding communities. For example, many community members in England's scenic Lake District strongly object to a twenty-seven-turbine wind farm planned just outside a national park. "This is a high-quality landscape. They shouldn't be putting those things in here,"[34] says one resident.

The debate over wind power has, for the first time, made opponents out of groups that previously agreed on environmental matters. Most national environmental groups such as Greenpeace and the Sierra Club strongly support wind and other non-fossil-fuel energy sources. "The broader environmental movement knows we have this urgent need for renewable energy to avert global warming,"[35] explains John Passacantando, executive director of Greenpeace USA. However, many environmentalists have protested wind projects proposed for areas they treasure for recreational opportunities and scenic beauty.

One battle currently in the spotlight is the Cape Wind project, a proposed wind farm of 130 turbines off the shore of Cape Cod. This project would be the first offshore wind farm in the United States and would provide 75 percent of the electricity needed by Cape Cod and nearby islands. The project has faced great opposition from many residents, including some staunch environmentalists such as Senator Ted Kennedy, who has a home in the area. Opponents of the project say that it will ruin the scenery and poses a danger to the environment and the local fishing industry. Supporters of the project within the environmental community are bothered by such a response. "There's no free lunch. 'Not in my backyard' is not environmentalism,"[36] says Paul Hansen, executive director of the Izaak Walton League of America, a conservation organization.

Some environmentalists view the debate over alternative energy sources as a signal of a shift in the philosophy of conservation from protecting individual places to protecting the planet. They acknowledge this change will be difficult. "We've always been a place-based organization, protecting places, but protecting our climate is just looking at it from a different angle and a different elevation,"[37] says the Sierra Club's David Hamilton. For some people, such as Arthur Larrivee, a homeowner in Massachusetts who installed two wind turbines in his backyard to power his home, the issue is not complicated at all. "The wind is blowing all day long and it's free," he says. "Why shouldn't I use it?"[38]

Power from Water

Another source of renewable energy is that generated by the movement of water, known as hydropower. Anyone watching

Power created by diverting rivers and building dams often comes at a significant cost to the environment.

the rushing of a river or the crashing of waves onto the seashore has witnessed the power that moving water can create. People have been using hydropower since the beginning of recorded history, usually by damming or diverting the flow of rivers. In modern times, the flow of water is directed through rotating turbines to produce clean and renewable electricity. Hydroelectric power from dams currently provides about 10 percent of the energy supply in the United States.

Power created by diverting rivers and building dams, however, often comes at a significant cost to the environment. When the flow of a river is altered, the entire ecosystem is affected. It becomes difficult or impossible for fish and other wildlife to travel past dams that block historic migration routes. Habitat downstream from a dam changes drastically with decreased or sporadic water flows. The creation of a dam also floods entire valleys, displacing wildlife and destroying habitat.

Going with the Flow

Because of their associated environmental concerns, traditional hydroelectric power projects have been waning in acceptance, and it is unlikely that any new hydroelectric plants will be built. In their place other, more innovative ways to harness the power of water are being explored. Instead of looking to rivers for power, scientists are now experimenting with using the tremendous force created by the movement of ocean waves and tides to produce electricity. The energy potential of the ocean is great—engineers estimate that capturing just 0.2 percent of the ocean's power would meet the entire planet's energy needs.

Scientists are testing nearly two dozen strategies for capturing energy from ocean waves. One system is the use of giant 17-ton floating buoys (15,422kg) made of strong magnets surrounded by coils of copper wire. The buoy's magnet is anchored to the seafloor and remains roughly in one position. The outer coil, however, bobs up and down with the motion of the waves. Electricity is generated as the magnet moves through the center of the copper coil. Cables carry the electric current to power substations on land for distribution.

EARTH IS A HEAT ENGINE

"We're literally riding around in space on a heat engine. If we can find an economical way to tap it, we can have nonpolluting energy from here to infinity."

—David N. Anderson, executive director,
Geothermal Resources Council

Quoted in John J. Berger, *Charging Ahead.* New York: Holt, 1997, p. 219.

The first wave-power projects in the United States using buoy technology are being tested on the West Coast, home to huge Pacific Ocean swells. "Oregon is the sweet spot for wave energy in the world," says Annette von Jouanne, an Oregon State University professor heading a wave energy project. "Anyone who goes to the coast can see the potential in that ocean."[37] The energy gained from two hundred buoys would provide enough electricity to power the city of Portland.

Another device developed to capture wave energy has a completely different design. The Pelamis, or sea snake, is a 450-foot-long steel tube (137m) made up of hinged segments. The train-sized snake is moored to the ocean floor at both ends. As the jointed segments move back and forth in the waves, the motion pushes pistons that drive electricity generators. The electricity is sent to shore through underwater cables. Pelamis has undergone extensive testing off the Scottish coast and has proven capable of holding up to the punishment of stormy seas, often the downfall of wave generators. The device's inventor estimates that a forty-sea-snake spread of 250 acres (101ha) could supply enough electricity to power twenty thousand homes. The world's first commercial wave power system, installed off the north coast of Portugal, uses Pelamis snakes. Other wave generators are being tested off the shores of New Jersey, Hawaii, England, and Australia.

Engineers involved in testing wave generators find considerable promise in the technology. Waves are much more consistent than wind and hold significantly more power in a concentrated area. Wave machines also leave a much smaller mark on the landscape. They are quiet, do not block views, and require much less space than wind farms. Although they could pose a hazard to ships if not clearly marked or placed outside of shipping lanes, they pose little threat to marine wildlife. Stephen Salter of the University of Edinburgh says wave machines like the sea snake are "quite nice to have around, just like big, friendly whales."[38]

Harnessing the Tide

Another way to get power from the sea is to take advantage of the large volume of moving water during tidal flows. Tidal power generators are usually underwater turbines that create electricity as the water flows in and out with the changing tides. The strength of tides varies a great deal around the world. Strongest tidal flows usually occur where narrow gaps in land formations funnel large amounts of water through a small area. In North America some of the best potential sites for tidal turbines are Nova Scotia's Bay of Fundy, Alaska's Knik Arm, and the entrance to San Francisco Bay.

A turbine generator in the Geysers geothermal plant in Middletown, California. This plant has produced electricity commercially since 1967.

Energy officials in Washington State are actively studying several sites for their tidal turbine potential. One site under consideration for a pilot project is Puget Sound's Tacoma Narrows. Powerful tides rushing through this channel have the potential to spin 64 underwater turbines to power 11,000 homes. The effects of tidal turbines on fish and other wildlife in Puget Sound and elsewhere are currently unknown and will require study. Many questions remain about the prospects of harnessing the ocean's power for wide-scale energy production. Most scientists involved in the research, however, are optimistic. John W. Griffiths, a renewable-energy consultant, has confidence in the promise of ocean power. "The situation is very similar to wind 15 years ago," he says. "We think that this is an industry waiting to happen."[39]

Geothermal Power

An alternative energy industry that is already well established is geothermal power. Geothermal power uses heat generated from deep within the earth's core. Geothermal power is most easily

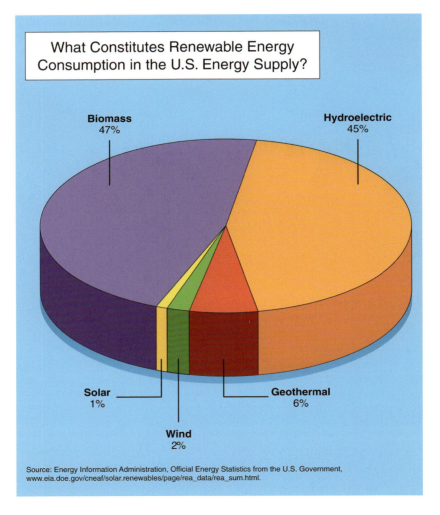

What Constitutes Renewable Energy Consumption in the U.S. Energy Supply?

Biomass 47%

Hydroelectric 45%

Solar 1%

Geothermal 6%

Wind 2%

Source: Energy Information Administration, Official Energy Statistics from the U.S. Government, www.eia.doe.gov/cneaf/solar.renewables/page/rea_data/rea_sum.html.

accessible in parts of the world with volcanic activity. In these places, heat from the earth's core rises through fissures, or deep cracks in the earth's surface, to reach the surface, where it heats rocks and water.

The resulting hot water is used to power geothermal plants. Geothermal plants generate electricity by using steam from hot water to drive turbines. The world's largest geothermal power plant is near San Francisco. The plant, called the Geysers, has produced electricity commercially since 1967. It gets its steam from 246 wells drilled as far as 2.5 miles (4km) into the rock.

Geothermal Potential

Author John J. Berger has studied the potential for renewable energy growth in the United States. He states that if technology advances, one day environmentally friendly geothermal power could supply all the energy America would ever need. For now, however, this energy potential is largely untapped, mostly due to a lack of research funding and the availability of cheaper fossil fuels. Berger acknowledges that no one knows how much power is available from geothermal sources. Says Berger: "By one estimate, geothermal resources exceed the world's entire coal, oil, and natural gas resources by 30 times. Another estimate found the heat content of the Earth's crust is hundreds of thousands of times U.S. annual energy demand."

John J. Berger, *Charging Ahead*. New York: Holt, 1997, pp. 234–35.

Stainless steel pipelines carry steam from the Geysers area to the Calpine geothermal plant in Middletown, California.

Water and steam emerge from the well at temperatures between 250°F and 700°F (120°C and 370°C). The Geysers uses this hot water to produce enough electricity to power almost all of San Francisco.

Geothermal plants in the western United States generate nearly 3,000 megawatts of power, more than twice the energy from solar and wind combined. The U.S. Department of Energy estimates that this geothermal energy prevents the emission of 22 million tons (20 billion kg) of carbon dioxide every year. Worldwide, geothermal plants provide power for over 60 million people. Many European countries utilize geothermal power for agriculture. Hot water from geothermal wells is pumped through pipes in greenhouses to grow a variety of crops. In Asia and the United States, geothermal heat is used widely in aquaculture, heating water for raising such diverse creatures as eels, shellfish, alligators, and tropical pet fish.

The most common use of geothermal power is as a direct heat source. Hot water from the ground is pumped through pipes for heating buildings. Some communities, such as Boise, Idaho, and Reykjavik, Iceland, already use direct geothermal heat extensively. In fact, nearly all buildings in Iceland's capital are heated through geothermal sources, making it one of the world's cleanest cities. In the future, geothermal power is expected to become more enticing to many other communities struggling with the problems of pollution and growing energy demands.

CHAPTER 5

THE NUCLEAR OPTION

The quest to develop new options for replacing fossil fuels has led to much debate between proponents of the various alternative energy sources. No source, however, is more intensely debated than nuclear power. Some people consider nuclear power to be a clean, safe, and affordable way to meet the world's growing energy needs. Others, however, strongly object to the use of nuclear energy due to concerns about power plant safety, the storage of dangerous nuclear wastes, and the potential for nuclear materials to be used as weapons.

What Is Nuclear Power?

In order to evaluate both sides of the nuclear argument, it is important to understand the basics of how nuclear power is produced. It is called nuclear power because the energy is created when the nucleus at the center of an atom is split in a process called nuclear fission. Nuclear fission uses the element uranium as fuel. Uranium is a fairly common element on earth, originating from the remains of shattered stars present when the planet was formed. The nuclei of certain kinds of uranium atoms (called U-235) are unstable and split easily. When a uranium nucleus is split, a great deal of energy is released in the form of heat.

Nuclear reactors work by controlling the fission, or splitting, of uranium atoms. The uranium fuel is formed into small pellets that are arranged into long rods inside the reactor. The uranium fuel rods are inserted into a water-filled chamber called the reactor core. Once inside the core, the uranium is bombarded with

The interior of a nuclear reactor at the Vermont Yankee nuclear power plant. With the containment cover removed, fuel rods can be seen beneath the water.

particles called neutrons. When a neutron collides with a uranium nucleus, the nucleus breaks up, releasing more neutrons. When some of these neutrons hit another uranium nucleus, that atom will also break apart and release even more neutrons. Some of these neutrons strike still more uranium atoms, splitting those as well. This process is called a chain reaction.

If a chain reaction continued uncontrolled, the uranium would create so much heat that it would melt. To prevent this, the fuel rods are separated by control rods that are made of a material that absorbs neutrons. Reactor operators raise or lower the control rods to manage the rate of the chain reaction. To create more heat, the control rods are raised, allowing more uranium to be bombarded by neutrons. To diminish the heat, the control rods are lowered between the fuel rods to absorb neutrons and slow the reaction. The water in the core also cools the uranium and assists in slowing the reaction.

The heat produced by the chain reaction boils the water in the reactor, turning it into steam. Just as in conventional coal-fired power plants, the steam runs through a turbine, causing it to spin a generator that produces electricity. The steam is then cooled in the nuclear plant's large cooling towers before being recirculated back to the core for reheating.

Nuclear Fears

Using a nuclear chain reaction to generate energy was considered an idea with great potential when the first commercial reactor was installed in Pennsylvania in 1957. The 1960s and 1970s saw a wave of nuclear power plant construction; by 1979 there were 107 reactors operating in the United States, producing 11 percent of the nation's electricity. Despite this growth in nuclear power, there was also a growing antinuclear movement. Many people were increasingly concerned about the public and environmental safety issues surrounding nuclear energy.

Some of the biggest fears about nuclear energy concern radiation. Radiation is energy given off from the nucleus of an atom. Radiation occurs naturally; it comes from the sun, stars, rocks, and soil. Radiation is also used in microwaves, X-rays, and medical treatments for cancer. However, a different type of radiation is released during the production of nuclear energy. Exposure to high levels of this type of radiation can damage the body's cells, leading to organ failure and cancer. Nuclear power plants are designed to prevent any dangerous radiation from escaping. A thick dome of steel and concrete, called the containment vessel, encases the reactor core to keep all the radiation inside.

AFRAID OF RADIATION

"Most Americans think they know about radiation because of Chernobyl, science fiction or the three-eyed fish in *The Simpsons*. So as a country, we are phobic about radiation."

—Ray Golden, spokesperson for Southern California
Edison's San Onofre nuclear generating station

Quoted in Judith Lewis, "Green to the Core? Part 1," *LA Weekly*, November 10, 2005. www.laweekly.com/general/features/green-to-the-core-part-1/151/.

Nuclear Accidents

Despite the safeguards in place, early opponents of nuclear power plants feared that an accident inside the core could cause the uranium to melt through the reactor and release radiation into the outside world. These fears were nearly realized on March 28, 1979, at the Three Mile Island nuclear power plant near Harrisburg, Pennsylvania. During operations, a valve became stuck open, causing water to drain from the reactor core. With the fuel rods partially uncovered, the temperature in the core rose to at least 4,800°F (2,649°C), nearly the heat required to cause the uranium to melt. Had a meltdown occurred, an explosion could have resulted that would have released large amounts of radiation into the atmosphere. Engineers were able to gain control of the plant's reactor, no one was killed or injured in the accident, and only a very small amount of radiation was released, but the event greatly heightened America's nuclear fears.

Chernobyl

Another much more serious accident occurred April 26, 1986, at the Chernobyl nuclear power plant in the former Soviet

Several technicians and Atomic Energy Commission officials watch as the reactor core is lowered into place at the Shippingport, Pennsylvania, nuclear power plant on October 6, 1957.

View of the Chernobyl nuclear power plant just days after the accident in 1986. The radioactive fallout from the Chernobyl explosion was carried by the wind thousands of miles over Asia and Europe, where it contaminated soil and agricultural crops.

Union (now Ukraine). Without warning, the reactor core exploded, blowing the top off the reactor and igniting a raging fire. With no special training on dealing with a reactor fire, firefighters poured water onto the blazing core. When the water hit the melting uranium, it billowed back up into the sky as radioactive steam. This radioactive fallout was carried by the wind thousands of miles over Asia and Europe, where it contaminated soil and agricultural crops.

Closer to the disaster site, the effects were catastrophic. Although the Soviet Union reported 31 deaths at the time of the accident, Ukraine officials now say more than 4,300 people were killed. At least another 6,00 people who worked to build a concrete case around the melted reactor have since died from radiation poisoning. As many as 375,000 people had to leave their homes because the area was so contaminated, leaving ghost towns behind. In addition, exposure to harmful doses of radiation may have affected as many as 17.5 million people in the region. The effects of nonlethal doses of radiation may take decades to become apparent in the form of health issues. As time passes, cancer rates among people downwind of the accident, especially children, continue to rise. In one town 120 miles (193km) from Chernobyl, all but 4 of the 200 school-age children have some form of radiation-related disease. A large number of babies with birth defects are now being born to women exposed to large doses of radiation at the time of the accident.

Opponents of nuclear power cite both the Chernobyl accident and the averted crisis at Three Mile Island, as well as less serious incidences that have occurred around the world, as strong evidence of the dangers of nuclear energy. These events strongly swayed the public's opinion against nuclear power. No new reactors have been built in the United States since 1985, and several have closed due to aging facilities. Many European countries have also decided against expanding their use of

The city of Pripyat, where fifty thousand people lived just two miles from Chernobyl, became a ghost town after the nuclear accident.

nuclear power in the face of protests and safety concerns. Proponents of nuclear power argue that the safety measures in place prevented the Three Mile Island accident from escalating. They also point out that reactors such as the one at Chernobyl, built by the former Soviet Union, fall below Western standards of safety, including the lack of a concrete containment dome surrounding the core.

Pushing for a Nuclear Comeback

Despite the problems suffered by the nuclear industry, nuclear power continues to play a role in helping the world meet its need for electricity. The United States is still the biggest total consumer of nuclear power; as of 2005, 103 reactors provided 19 percent of the nation's electricity. Worldwide, 442 reactors in 30 countries meet 16 percent of electricity demand. France gets 78 percent of its electricity from nuclear power, far more than any other country. Some countries, such as China, India, and Japan, plan to greatly increase their use of nuclear power by 2020. Not all countries are embracing the use of nuclear power, however. Because of the safety concerns of radiation and the risk of accidents, the United States, the United Kingdom, Germany, and Russia plan significant reductions in nuclear power generation. Sweden and the Netherlands plan to phase out nuclear power completely over the coming decades.

While some countries are backing away from nuclear power, others are pushing for giving the technology a fresh look. In fact, even some staunch environmentalists, long opposed to nuclear power, are reconsidering their position in light of nuclear power's potential for reducing the world's dependence on fossil fuels. This surprising shift in attitude is driven mostly by a desire to halt the serious consequences of climate change caused by the burning of coal and petroleum products.

Patrick Moore, a longtime environmentalist, explains his new take on nuclear power:

> In the early 1970s when I helped found Greenpeace, I believed that nuclear energy was synonymous with nuclear holocaust, as did most of my compatriots. . . . Thirty years on, my views have changed, and the rest of

the environmental movement needs to update its views, too, because nuclear energy may just be the energy source that can save our planet from another possible disaster: catastrophic climate change.[40]

Moore points to the fact that the emissions from coal-fired power plants in the United States produce nearly 2 billion tons (1.8 trillion kg) of carbon dioxide each year—the same amount as the exhaust from 300 million cars. Nuclear power creates no carbon dioxide emissions. The 103 nuclear power plants operating in the United States avoid giving off the amount of carbon dioxide that would be produced by 100 million cars.

GLOBAL WARMING VS. NUCLEAR POWER

"Is it possible that we have come to this: a choice between a catastrophic warming trend and the most feared energy source on earth?"

—Judith Lewis

Judith Lewis, "Green to the Core? Part 1," *LA Weekly*, November 10, 2005. www. laweekly. com/general/features/green-to-the-core-part-1/151/.

The environmentalists who now endorse taking a closer look at nuclear power admit the technology does pose serious potential safety issues, but that their paramount concern is quickly stemming the tide of global greenhouse gas release. James Lovelock, a prominent environmentalist supporting the expansion of nuclear energy, insists:

We can not continue drawing energy from fossil fuels and there is no chance that the renewables, wind, tide and water power can provide enough energy and in time. If we had 50 years or more we might make these our main sources. But we do not have 50 years; the Earth is already so disabled by the insidious poison of greenhouse gases that even if we stop all fossil fuel burning immediately, the consequences of what we have already done will last for 1,000 years. Every year that we continue burning carbon makes it worse for our descendants and for civilization.[41]

Nuclear Opposition

While some environmentalists support the carbon-free energy provided by nuclear power, there are many others who believe the benefits are not worth the risk and support advancing other alternative energy sources instead. In 2005 a group of over three hundred organizations, including Greenpeace, Friends of the Earth, and the Sierra Club, issued a position statement on nuclear power. In it, they "flatly reject the argument that increased investment in nuclear capacity is an acceptable or necessary solution." They also voice concern that spending money to develop nuclear power is "displacing the resources needed to ensure a real solution to the global warming issue."[42]

Some nuclear opponents are more blunt about the inherent risks of using nuclear power. "The nuclear industry is a cancer industry," says Dr. Helen Caldicott, a longtime antinuclear activist. "Nuclear power is going to induce millions of cases of cancer, particularly in children who are so radiosensitive. And it causes genetic disease, not just in humans but also in other creatures. So it's an evil industry,

Many environmentalists believe the benefits of nuclear power are not worth the risks, such as contamination from mishandled containers, and support advancing other alternative energy sources instead.

Nuclear Fusion

Scientists are researching another type of nuclear reaction they believe may hold promise as a limitless energy source in the future. Seemingly out of science fiction, nuclear fusion replicates the process that powers the sun. Instead of splitting the nuclei of atoms, as takes place in nuclear fission, fusion causes nuclei to collide, also resulting in the release of energy. Fusion is considered a very attractive alternative to fission since it requires no radioactive elements and produces no radioactive waste. Instead, it uses the abundant element hydrogen as fuel.

The drawback to nuclear fusion is that is requires high pressure and extremely high temperatures of up to 212 million° F (118 million° C). A group of scientists from thirty countries are working together to develop a fusion reactor that uses a ring of powerful magnets to trigger the reaction. So far, experiments have fused hydrogen nuclei, but only for a few seconds. The experiment also required a great deal more energy than the fusion released. Because the physics of fusion are well understood, many researchers believe it will eventually be controlled. However, it is expected to take several decades and great cost before a commercial fusion reactor is available.

medically speaking."[43] A 1991 National Cancer Institute study of people living near nuclear facilities, however, shows no increase in cancer death rates in that population. Critics of nuclear power also voice concerns that reactors are prime terrorist targets and that radioactive materials might be used for making weapons of mass destruction.

James Lovelock counters these arguments. "Opposition to nuclear energy is based on irrational fear fed by Hollywood-style fiction, the Green lobbies and the media. These fears are unjustified, and nuclear energy from its start in 1952 has proved to be the safest of all energy sources."[44] No deaths have ever been attributed to radiation in the history of commercial nuclear power in the United States. However, more than five thousand coal mining–related deaths occur worldwide every year.

Los Angeles Times columnist George Monbiot also argues that the threat of terrorism pales when compared to global warming. "Although the radiation released by accidents or terrorists could kill hundreds or perhaps thousands of people, climate change caused by burning fossil fuels threatens hundreds of millions,"[45] he says. Environmentalist Stewart Brand agrees. "How many Chernobyls equal one abrupt climate change? A climate change where the Gulf Stream turns off, and not only Europe but the whole world gets much colder, drier and windier, and the Earth then drops its carrying capacity by 20 or 40 percent?"[46] he asks.

The Challenge of Nuclear Waste

While disagreement persists about the dangers of nuclear power, both sides recognize the troubling challenge of handling and storing nuclear waste. Hazardous radioactive waste material is produced at all stages of the nuclear process, from mining the uranium to the operation of a nuclear power plant. These wastes must be stored in such a manner that the radiation cannot escape and harm people and the environment.

NUCLEAR WASTE BETTER THAN ALTERNATIVE

"Radioactive wastes are a challenge. But burdening future generations with nuclear wastes in deep shafts is probably more reasonable than burdening them with a warmer world in which Manhattan is submerged under 20 feet of water."

—Nicholas D. Kristof

Nicholas D. Kristof, "Nukes Are Green," *New York Times*, April 9, 2005. www.nytimes. com/2005/04/09/opinion/09kristof.html.

Not all radioactive waste is equally dangerous. Low-level waste includes uranium mining tools, lab equipment, and clothing worn by workers. More dangerous are materials that have come in contact with uranium fuel, such as fuel transport containers. These types of wastes can be stored in buried or concrete-encased metal drums. The most dangerous, or high-level, waste is the uranium fuel itself. Fuel rods can power fission reactions for one to three years, after which time they are removed from the core. Some of the uranium can be reprocessed into new fuel, although this process is not yet permitted in the United States due to safety concerns. Spent fuel rods are extremely hot from the fission reactions and must be stored in water until they cool. These fuel rods will continue to give off radiation for tens of thousands of years. So far, no one has discovered a safe way to store this waste that will guarantee it stays secure for such a long time period.

Commercial nuclear power plants produce 3,000 tons (2.72 million kg) of high-level waste each year, most of which is maintained in temporary storage facilities at nuclear power plants across the country. As the waste piles up, the U.S. government continues to work on a solution for its permanent disposal. Since 1982 the Department of Energy has been developing a plan to bury the waste deep underground at the Yucca Mountain Repository in Nevada. Originally scheduled to open in 1998, the Yucca Mountain site has been plagued with problems, including resistance from Nevada officials and concerns about the possibility that waste will eventually leak from storage containers. Construction of the site has already cost $9 billion. Robin Becker, executive director of the Alliance for Nuclear Responsibility, believes the investment in nuclear waste storage could be better spent on developing other energy sources. "If

Workers at the Yucca Mountain nuclear waste repository in Nevada. Numerous legal challenges against the site have delayed its opening to accept nuclear materials.

Nuclear Fuel Reprocessing

One way that France, Russia, and Japan cope with the issue of nuclear waste is through the reprocessing of fuel rods. After completing fission reactions, the fuel rods contain many elements such as depleted uranium and plutonium that can be recovered and reused. These are the most radioactive products of fission. The remaining nuclear waste has much lower levels of radiation and loses 99 percent of its radioactivity in six hundred years (versus potentially a million years for plutonium). Reprocessing fuel rods also reduces the amount of waste needing storage by 95 percent.

Although reprocessing is commonly done overseas, the United States has discontinued the practice since 1977 because of fears that the resulting plutonium could be stolen and provide fuel for nuclear weapons. In fact, there are already U.S. supplies of plutonium that are unaccounted for. However, given the issues surrounding nuclear waste storage, the United States is once again gearing up to begin reprocessing. A reprocessing plant is in development in South Carolina, and the United States is part of a partnership with other countries to reprocess spent fuel.

Extremely strict regulations must be followed to ensure safe handling of such hazardous materials. Reprocessing in the United States has a poor track record, including leakage of high-level liquid waste from a plutonium reprocessing plant in Hanford, Washington. These problems must be overcome in order to safely recover spent nuclear fuel and reduce dangerous nuclear waste.

the same investment in dollars were made in renewable, we would go from being the laughingstock to a leader in renewable energy,"[47] she says.

Some nuclear proponents express frustration at the government's slow pace of coming to terms with dealing with nuclear waste. According to some, waste should be dealt with the best way possible with current technology; worrying about developing a foolproof system to contain radiation for ten thousand years is tomorrow's concern. Stewart Brand believes that leaving the burden of nuclear waste is "way, way different than losing species you can't get back. This is passing on an engineering problem to future generations. And that is fair to do."[48]

Accepting Nuclear Power

While the idea of accepting nuclear power is slowly growing in the United States, it has much stronger public support in parts of Europe and Asia. A 2005 European poll found 60 percent of people surveyed believed that nuclear power was a climate-friendly alternative to oil. Part of the reason for this response may lie with the openness with which some other countries have typically treated the nuclear industry. In the United States there has been little emphasis given to educating the public on nuclear issues. Additionally, because the government has been slow to reveal information on nuclear accidents and waste issues, the public tends to be suspicious and distrustful of the industry. In contrast, French and Japanese nuclear plants have on-site science centers that students visit on field trips to learn about the nuclear process.

RIGHT TO FEAR NUCLEAR ENERGY

"Would you allow your child to play in the park if there were a poisonous snake loose somewhere within it, however tiny the probability of being bitten? What if the snake were invisible, and its bite caused cancer or leukemia? . . . It is time to outlaw nuclear pollution. We are right to be frightened of invisible snakes."

—Chris Busby

Chris Busby, "The Thames Valley: A Radioactive Breeding Ground for Cancer," *Ecologist,* September/October 1997.

Some experts believe that an aggressive education campaign is necessary for the American public to understand better and to accept nuclear power. In his 2005 energy policy, President Bush called for a return to nuclear power plant construction as one way to address climate change and foster the country's energy independence. According to Greenpeace, this approach is misguided. "Nuclear power will fail to address climate change for the same reason it has failed to stem the flow of foreign oil. Nuclear power generates electricity and electricity does not power our automobiles."[49]

CHAPTER 6

THE FUTURE OF ENERGY

As the planet's population continues to grow and developing countries improve their standards of living, worldwide demand for energy is expected to quickly escalate. The International Energy Agency estimates that in the next thirty years, demand for energy will increase by nearly two-thirds. Not only is the ability to supply this demand into the future with fossil fuels uncertain, but the resulting increase in pollution and greenhouse gas emissions may also have serious, permanent effects on people and the environment. But can the world's growing energy needs be met using clean, alternative sources?

NO POWER IS CHEAP POWER

"I call it 'negawatts.' There's no cheaper or cleaner power than the power you don't produce."

—Amory Lovins of the Rocky Mountain Institute,
referring to energy conservation

Quoted in Tom Clynes, "The Energy 10 Step to End America's Fossil Fuel Addiction," *Popular Science*, July 2006. www.popsci.com/popsci/energy/d5c81e69921ab010vgn vcm1000004eecbccdrcrd.html.

Fossil fuels are unlikely to have a single, dominant replacement. Most energy experts agree that there is no magic solution just around the corner that will meet the world's energy needs. Instead, they predict a new global energy system in which diverse fuel sources work together to provide clean, abundant energy. In addition, this new system will have an increasing reliance on energy efficiency and conservation.

Green Power

Support for this type of hybrid system is already gathering momentum. Power generated through the use of environmentally friendly technology such as solar and wind power is sold under the label of "green power." Individual consumers and businesses can often sign up with their local power companies to purchase green power to provide a portion of their electricity needs. Purchasers of green power pay slightly more for their power to cover the higher cost of the alternatives. But by choosing to buy green power, they provide a market to support the development of alternative energy sources.

The number of consumers choosing to enroll in green power programs is growing. One study of green power programs in the Northwest showed that over one hundred thousand consumers in the region paid a premium to their power companies for alternative energy in 2005, an 18 percent increase from the year before. This amount of green power purchased avoided over 1 billion pounds (454 million kg) of carbon dioxide emissions that would have resulted if the electricity had been produced in a traditional power plant. Although green power participation rates may be growing, they still represent a very small portion of electricity sales. Only 5.3 percent of Portland General Electric customers participated in the program in 2005, although that

(From left) actors Ted Danson, Ed Begley Jr., Wendie Malick, Los Angeles Department of Water and Power general manager S. David Freeman, and actor Beau Bridges help launch the "Green Power for a Green LA" program in 1999 with the goal of bringing alternative energy sources to the consumer.

utility sells the largest percentage of green power in the region. In fact, half of all electricity customers in the United States have the option to enroll in green power programs, yet only about five hundred thousand had done so by the end of 2005. Europeans have been quicker to support green power. By 2004 there were nearly 3 million green power consumers in the Netherlands alone.

A Vision for an Alternative Energy Future

Encouraging individuals and businesses to turn to renewable energy sources is just the beginning of what some advocates hope will become a green energy revolution. One part of this revolution is led by a coalition of mayors from across the country. In 2005 Seattle mayor Greg Nickels launched the U.S. Mayors' Climate Protection Agreement to develop a program for cities to cut global warming emissions to below 1990 levels by 2012. As of February 2007, 407 mayors in fifty states had signed on, agreeing to invest in renewable energy and alternative fuels and to reduce their cities' polluting emissions.

PEOPLE DON'T UNDERSTAND ELECTRICITY

"There's an immense and, at times, willful ignorance in America about what goes on behind the light switch. Nowadays, people can tell you exactly what they paid for their last gallon of gas, but they're clueless when it comes to electricity. Most people don't know what a kilowatt is, let alone what it costs."

—Jeff Goodell

Quoted in Nelson Harvey, "The Real Black Gold," *American Prospect,* June 13, 2006. www.prospect.org/web/page.ww?section=root&name=ViewWeb&articleId=11631.

One big step toward achieving the program's goals is reducing citizens' dependence on cars by developing better public transportation systems. In Seattle that means the creation of new light rail and bus routes and discouraging drivers by raising parking rates. This shift will be expensive and require a great deal of public education. Despite the hurdles, Mayor Nickels is optimistic that his city will lead the way. "When it comes to climate change, we are all

Building Green

Cities around the United States are becoming greener by adopting building practices that meet the standards of the U.S. Green Building Council's Leadership in Energy and Environmental Design program (LEED). The LEED rating system provides buildings with different levels of green certification based on an environmental scorecard of their construction and operation. To become LEED certified, buildings are evaluated in key areas relating to the building's human and environmental health, including energy efficiency, the use of environmentally friendly building materials, indoor environmental quality, and water savings.

Many cities across the country, including Atlanta, Dallas, and Chicago, have requirements that new buildings over a certain size must meet at least a LEED silver certification. San Francisco was one of the first cities to adopt green building practices for city construction projects and now requires all new construction to meet green building standards. Through this practice, the city has shown that green building is not difficult. Mark Palmer, San Francisco's green building coordinator, is proud that the city is setting an example. "We want to show that we're just not telling people what they should do, but also prove we can do it ourselves," he says.

Quoted in *Buildings,* "America's Cities 'LEED' the Way," May 2005. www.buildings.com/Articles/detail.asp?ArticleID=2475.

part of the problem—and part of the solution," he says. "Together we can make Seattle the most climate-friendly city in the country."[50] Mayor Nickels's spokesperson believes that Seattle's environmentally friendly track record is encouraging. "If we can't do it here," he says, "it's hard to imagine doing it elsewhere."[51]

Energy Conservation

Cities will make significant headway into reducing their production of climate-changing pollutants by using energy alternatives and increasing the use of public transportation. However, another way to reduce the need for fossil fuels is through energy conservation. Energy can be conserved in two ways. One way is when people change their behavior in order to use less energy, such as by turning down the heater thermostats in their homes. Another way is by increasing the efficiency of machines that use power. Increasing

Compact fluorescent lamps (CFL) turn 25 percent of the energy they use into light.

efficiency means using less power to do more work. In fact, the U.S. Department of Energy estimates that increasing energy efficiency could reduce energy use in the country by 20 percent by 2020.

Technology has allowed for rapid advances in the efficiency of everything from lightbulbs to power plants. An incandescent lightbulb, for example, turns only 5 percent of the electricity it consumes into light, giving off the remainder as heat. Fluorescent bulbs are more efficient, turning 25 percent of the energy they use into light. Researchers, however, are now looking to replace these older light sources with a new generation of light emitting diodes (LEDs) such as those found in digital clocks, which have an efficiency of 50 percent. The Energy Department estimates that widespread use of LEDs could cut the amount of electricity the country uses for lighting in half, saving $30 billion in fuel costs and significant amounts of pollution each year.

The Energy Efficiency Paradox

Because vehicles account for the greatest consumption of fossil fuels, increasing the efficiency of cars is usually seen as having a significant impact on reducing oil use. Automakers are looking at a variety of means for making cars more efficient. In addition to finding more fuel-efficient energy sources, automakers are experimenting with lightweight metals and plastics that increase efficiency while still providing the strength needed for safety.

The efficiency of automobiles sold in the United States has increased since the 1980s, but those gains have been completely offset by the increasing number of miles Americans drive. Part of the problem lies with the relatively low price of gasoline and diesel fuel. Although consumers protest when fuel prices rise, the United States actually has some of the lowest gas prices in the world—one-half to one-third lower than in many European countries. These low prices, combined with the high cost and low availability of alternative fuels, give Americans little financial incentive to conserve.

Overall, the energy efficiency of the United States has improved by about one-third in the last twenty years. However, in that same time period, instead of energy use declining it has actually increased by 25 percent. This trend is sometimes called the "efficiency paradox." Part of the gain may be the result of a growing population, but author William Sweet believes another major factor is the fact that when "people are given a more energy-efficient way of doing something, they almost always do it more."[52] So instead of energy efficiency leading to conservation, it leads to increased resource use.

The same pattern of energy used for American transportation can be seen in energy used in American homes. There is now a multitude of energy-saving features built into new homes that have significantly reduced their square-foot energy needs over the past few decades. However, American home size has increased by 50 percent in the same time period; homes now consume more total energy than ever.

Changing Energy Attitudes

Ironically, despite rising consumption levels, most Americans claim to be concerned about reducing use of fossil fuels. Ninety percent of people surveyed by the American Institute of Architects said they would be willing to pay four thousand dollars to five thousand dollars more for a house built to conserve energy. Many national polls show that a large majority of Americans are concerned by the looming threat of global climate change and political impacts of buying foreign oil. However, despite these changing attitudes, Americans bought twenty-three gas-guzzling SUVs for every one hybrid in 2005 and continue to build large vacation homes, adding to a growing total energy consumption.

Many energy industry observers believe a shake-up in American attitudes about energy is needed. Michael T. Klare, author of *Blood and Oil*, explains:

We are not likely to change our fundamental behavior—
to start relying less on conventional automobiles and
other oil-powered devices—unless there is a dramatic
change in national attitudes about individual and soci-
etal energy behavior. We need, in short, to undergo what
sociologists call a *paradigm shift*—a complete rethinking
of our basic outlook on this critical issue.[53]

Klare describes how people have experienced such attitude
shifts in the past; today, for example, the once-acceptable practice of smoking is banned in most public places.

A change in attitude that leads to conservation action will only
be possible if it is supported by changes in the other factors currently
contributing to America's oil addiction. These changes include
increasing public education about the consequences of continued
dependence on oil, such as global warming and health-threatening
pollution. A greater focus on the issue by state and national leaders
will also play an important role in increasing acceptance of conservation measures. Most important, however, will be the availability of
affordable and readily available energy alternatives.

Corporations Go Green

This attitude shift is beginning to occur among U.S. corporations. These companies are finding that incorporating energy-

*Many polls show that Americans are concerned by the looming threat of global climate
change and political impacts of buying foreign oil, like from this oil refinery in Saudi
Arabia.*

A New Way to Promote Renewable Energy

Thomas Starrs, former chair of the American Solar Energy Society, has given much thought to the apparent state of denial that most Americans are in regarding the need for energy alternatives. He has come to the conclusion that people have adopted a "head in the sand" approach due to fear of the personal sacrifices and scary challenges involved in living in a world without fossil fuels.

Instead of focusing on the consequences of climate change and energy shortages, Starrs recommends promoting the benefits of alternative energy instead. He suggests a gentler approach to persuade Americans to embrace the behavior changes needed.

The solution, it seems to me, is for renewable energy advocates to spend less time talking to our families, friends and neighbors about the dire consequences of continued fossil-fuel dependence, and more time talking about the extraordinary opportunities associated with a post-petroleum, renewable-fueled, sustainable energy future. We need to paint a picture of a prettier place, one that will be cleaner and safer for our children, and for our children's children.

Thomas Starrs, "It's a Beautiful (Post-petroleum) World," *Solar Today,* November/December 2005. www. solartoday.org/2005/nov_dec05/Chairs_Corner_ ND05_Starrs. pdf.

conserving practices into their business plans not only develops goodwill within their communities, but also benefits the company's bottom line. In October 2006 Wells Fargo and Company became the largest corporate purchaser of green power. The banking company will use wind energy to power 40 percent of their electricity use, preventing the emissions equivalent of 40 million gallons (151 million l) of gasoline. Among the other companies listed on the Environmental Protection Agency's list of the top twenty-five purchasers of green power are Whole Foods Market (which gets 100 percent of its power from renewables), Johnson & Johnson, Starbucks, and Sprint Nextel.

The world's number one retailer, Wal-Mart, is also going green in a big way. The company plans to invest $500 million a year in developing energy-saving technologies and practices throughout its enormous retailing empire. Wal-Mart plans to double the efficiency of its trucking fleet, one of the largest in the country, by 2015 through the use of hybrid trucks and new lower-friction tires. The company is already saving $25 million a year in fuel costs just by having drivers turn off their engines when they take rest breaks.

Wal-Mart, the nation's largest private electricity user, has also pledged to reduce energy use by 30 percent in its seven thousand stores. It will achieve this by using energy-efficient LED lights, increasing the use of natural light through skylights in stores, and employing solar and wind power. The company is also rethinking the products it sells. It now encourages its suppliers to reduce packaging and manufacture more organic goods, strategies that decrease the energy required to produce and transport the products.

Lee Scott, Wal-Mart's CEO, acknowledges that some of the changes were undertaken in order to develop public feelings of goodwill toward the company. The effort, however, is now fueled by a sense of obligation to do the right thing for people and the planet. Scott says that as the company began to examine their impact on the planet, "what struck us was: this world is much more fragile than any of us would have thought years ago."[54]

Profits in Alternative Energy

Many other corporations are joining the push to go green. In addition to helping the environment, companies now view the fledgling alternative energy business as a market where there is the potential for significant profit. Investors expect companies that create alternative energy technologies and products to be one of the fastest growing areas of the business world. Elon Musk, cofounder of the online payment service PayPal, has started several companies based on technology that supports environmentally friendly energy, also known as clean technology. "Clean tech will be the biggest growth sector of the 21st century," he says. "Put it this way: Energy is way bigger than the Internet, and almost all of it will have to convert to renewable generation. That's a big deal."[55]

Many others from the Internet business community are embracing the rush toward clean energy technology. Internet entrepreneur Bill Gross is one of them. "Reinventing energy is a multitrillion-dollar opportunity. . . . It dwarfs any business opportunity in history."[56] Business investment in clean technology is growing fast. In fact, investment in products and services that increase energy efficiency was up 53 percent from 2005 to 2006. All of this investment is expected to lead to improvements in technology or even new breakthroughs, both of which could lower prices so alternative energy will be more readily available to consumers.

This new clean technology economy and actions by retailers like Wal-Mart may be the push consumers need to develop the attitude of conservation that many believe is currently lacking. Instead of using environmental protection arguments to influence people's behavior, lower prices and greater opportunities to purchase alternative energy products may achieve the same result. Kevin Danaher, organizer of the Green Festival, the world's largest environmental exposition, explains:

Honorees Willie Nelson and Daryl Hannah pose with presenters Woody Harrelson and Jon Lovitz at the 14th Annual Environmental Media Awards in 2004. Awards like this help recognize those who make a positive difference in the environment and encourage others to do so as well.

We're seeing a capital shift toward the green economy.
Toward an economy where there's two greens, this green
and the environmental green. Where you can make better profits protecting nature and saving nature and saving resources than you can destroying the environment.
And that's a seminal shift, we're going into a different
kind of economy.[57]

All of this progress toward a new alternative energy economy is an encouraging sign to environmentalists who have
worked on these issues for decades. They see the benefit of having corporate allies that may change the way the world does
business. "When you hear your words coming out of their
mouths, it's amazing," says Suzanne Apple of the World Wildlife
Fund. "These are issues we've been working on for years."[58]

The Future of Energy

It remains to be seen whether or not Americans and the rest of the
world will be able to wean themselves from their fossil fuel addiction in time. Environmentalist Amory Lovins believes the answer is
up to everyone to decide. "Our energy future is choice, not fate," he
says. "Oil dependence is a problem we need no longer have—and
it's cheaper not to. U.S. oil dependence can be eliminated by proven
and attractive technologies that create wealth, enhance choice, and
strengthen common security."[59]

Perhaps writer Michael Parfit best expresses the opinion of
many who predict a major shift in how the world gets and uses
energy. "The answers are out there. But they all require one more
thing of us humans who huddle around the fossil fuel fire: We're
going to have to make a big leap—toward a different kind of
world."[60]

NOTES

Introduction: Addicted to Oil

1. Quoted in White House, "State of the Union Address by the President," January 31, 2006. www.whitehouse.gov/state oftheunion/2006/index.html.

Chapter 1: In Pursuit of Energy Alternatives

2. Paul Roberts, *The End of Oil*. New York: Houghton Mifflin, 2004, p. 26.
3. Roberts, *The End of Oil*, p. 6.
4. Quoted in Roberts, *The End of Oil*, p. 52.
5. Quoted in Daniel A. Leone, ed., *Is the World Heading Toward an Energy Crisis?* Detroit: Thomson Gale, 2006, p. 6.
6. Quoted in Roberts, *The End of Oil*, pp. 51–52.
7. Kenneth Deffeyes, "It's the End of Oil," *Time*, October 31, 2005, p. 66.
8. Quoted in Roberts, *The End of Oil*, p. 56.
9. Quoted in *Economist*, "Steady as She Goes," April 22, 2006, pp. 66–67.
10. Roberts, *The End of Oil*, p. 65.
11. Quoted in Roberts, *The End of Oil*, p. 65.
12. Quoted in Roberts, *The End of Oil*, p. 65.
13. Quoted in Ross Gelbspan, "Michael Crichton's Misstated State of Fear," *National Wildlife*, April/May 2005, p. 12.
14. Al Gore, "The Time to Act Is Now," Salon.com, November 4, 2005. http://dir.salon.com/story/opinion/feature/2005/11/04/gore/index.html.
15. Patrick J. Michaels, "Is Global Warming Always Bad?" Cato Institute, November 7, 2004. www.cato.org/dailys/11-07-04.html.
16. Matthew Yeomans, *Oil*. New York: New Press, 2004, p. 121.
17. Quoted in Michael T. Klare, *Blood and Oil*. New York:

Metropolitan, 2004, p. 9.

18. Quoted in Yeomans, *Oil*, p. 27.

19. Klare, *Blood and Oil*, p. 7.

20. Quoted in Klare, *Blood and Oil*, p. 15.

21. Quoted in White House, "State of the Union Address by the President."

Chapter 2: Developing Alternative Vehicle Fuels

22. Quoted in Katharine Mieszkowski, "Can Hydrogen Save Us?" *Yes!* Fall 2004, p. 29.

23. Pamela Grossman, "Eulogizing the EV1: A Talk with Chris Paine, Director of Who Killed the Electric Car," *Seedmagazine.com*, June 30, 2006. http://seedmagazine.com/news/2006/06/eulogizing_the_ev1.php.

24. Quoted in Mike Musgrove, "It's Expensive, Fast, Stylish—and Electric?" *News Tribune*, July 23, 2006, p. A4.

25. Quoted in Michael Parfit, "Future Power," *National Geographic*, August 2005, pp. 22–23.

26. Quoted in John W. Schoen, "Rising Oil Prices Spark Interest in Biofuels," MSNBC.com, August 25, 2005. www.msnbc.msn.com/id/7549534/.

27. Quoted in David Welch and Adam Aston, "Fill 'Er Up—but with What?" *Business Week*, May 22, 2006, p. 60.

28. Kenneth S. Deffeyes, *Beyond Oil: The View from Hubbert's Peak*. New York: Hill and Wang, 2005, p. 153.

29. Quoted in Christine Woodside, *The Homeowner's Guide to Energy Independence*. Guilford, CT: Lyons, 2006, p. 64.

30. Quoted in Vijay V. Vaitheeswaran, *Power to the People*. New York: Farrar, Straus and Giroux, 2003, p. 255.

Chapter 3: What Is the Potential of Solar Power?

31. Quoted in Tom Clynes, "The Energy 10 Step to End America's Fossil Fuel Addiction," *Popular Science*, July 2006, p. 47.

32. Quoted in Toye Olori, "Nigeria: Solar Power Goes Where Rickety Power Grid Can't," *Global Information Network*, August 7, 2006, p. 1.

33. Ron Larson, "Renewable Energy and Energy Efficiency:

Something to Believe In," *Solar Today*, January/February 2006, p. 4.

Chapter 4: Harnessing Energy from the Earth

34. Quoted in Parfit, "Future Power," p. 19.
35. Quoted in Felicity Barringer, "Debate over Wind Power Creates Environmental Rift," *New York Times*, June 6, 2006, p. A18.
36. Quoted in Barringer, "Debate over Wind Power Creates Environmental Rift," p. A18.
37. Quoted in Associated Press, "OSU Researchers Hope to Ride Wave of Electricity," *Columbian*, April 30, 2006, p. C2.
38. Quoted in Eric Scigliano, "Waves, Not Oil," *Discover*, December 2005, p. 45.
39. Quoted in Heather Timmons, "A Renewable Source, and Clean, but Not Without Its Critics," *New York Times*, August 3, 2006, p. C1.

Chapter 5: The Nuclear Option

40. Patrick Moore, "Going Nuclear: A Green Makes the Case," *Washington Post*, April 16, 2006, p. B1.
41. James Lovelock, "Nuclear Power Is the Only Green Solution," *Independent*, May 24, 2004. www.ecolo.org/media/articles/articles.in.english/love-indep-24-05-04.htm.
42. Public Citizen, "Environmental Statement on Nuclear Energy and Global Warming," June 2005. www.citizen.org/documents/groupnuclearstmt.pdf.
43. Quoted in Judith Lewis, "Green to the Core? Part 1," *LA Weekly*, November 10, 2005. www.laweekly.com/general/features/green-to-the-core-part-1/151/.
44. Lovelock, "Nuclear Power Is the Only Green Solution."
45. George Monbiot, "Warming Up to Nuclear Power," *Los Angeles Times*, June 11, 2006, p. M1.
46. Quoted in Judith Lewis, "Green to the Core? Part 2," *LA Weekly*, November 10, 2005. www.laweekly.com/general/features/green-to-the-core-part-2/150/.
47. Quoted in Lewis, "Green to the Core? Part 2."
48. Quoted in Lewis, "Green to the Core? Part 2."

49. Greenpeace, "Nuclear Power's Extreme Makeover." www.greenpeace.org/usa/campaigns/nuclear/nuclear-power-s-extreme-makeov.

Chapter 6: The Future of Energy

50. Quoted in City of Seattle press release, "Mayor Launches Effort to Cut Seattle's Greenhouse Gas Emissions," September 27, 2006. www.seattle.gov/news/detail_print. asp?ID=6547&Dept=40.

51. Quoted in *E: The Environmental Magazine*, "Points of Light," July/August 2006, pp. 26-39, 62-63.

52. William Sweet, *Kicking the Carbon Habit*. New York: Columbia University Press, 2006, p. 163.

53. Klare, *Blood and Oil*, p. 187.

54. Quoted in Mindy Fetterman, "Wal-Mart Grows 'Green' Strategies," *USA Today*, September 25, 2006, p. A1.

55. Quoted in Joshua Davis, "Put Your Money Where the Green Is," *Outside*, November 2006, p. 104.

56. Quoted in Daniel Gross, "Vets of Dot-Com Boom-Bubble Move to Alternative Energy," *News Tribune*, July 30, 2006, Insight, p.4.

57. Quoted in "Going Green Goes Mainstream," CBS News, October 15, 2006. www.cbsnews.com/stories/2006/10/15/sunday/printable2090006.shtml.

58. Quoted in Fetterman, "Wal-Mart Grows 'Green' Strategies," p. A2.

59. Quoted in Steven Mufson, "One Man's Long Battle to Get U.S. to Kick Oil," *Washington Post*, July 25, 2006, p. D.1.

60. Parfit, "Future Power," p. 7.

Chapter 1: In Pursuit of Energy Alternatives

1. What does the author mean by an "energy economy?"

2. Why does Paul Roberts question whether the United States will have "the political will" to prepare for running out of oil?

3. Do you agree with Patrick Michael's position that scientists have little incentive to promote the positive aspects of their research findings?

4. What is the impact of America's dependence on imported oil?

Chapter 2: Developing Alternative Vehicle Fuels

1. What are some roadblocks to alternative fuels gaining broad public appeal?

2. Explain what Ryan Wiser means when he says, "There are many in the energy community who believe that the amount in the oil that you use to produce a gallon of ethanol is about the same as you get out of it once you've made it."

3. Why do you think the United States has lagged behind other countries in developing alternative fuels?

4. What alternative vehicle fuel do you believe holds the most promise? Why?

Chapter 3: What Is the Potential of Solar Power?

1. Why is solar power considered a more promising energy source than it was in the 1970s?

2. What are the primary challenges in developing solar power?

3. How do solar thermal systems differ from systems using solar (photovoltaic) cells?

4. Why have people in the United States been slow to accept solar power?

Chapter 4: Harnessing Energy from the Earth

1. Why is wind power an appropriate energy system for rural or isolated communities?

2. What does the author mean by "a shift in the philosophy of conservation from protecting individual places to protecting the planet?"

3. Describe the benefits and drawbacks of generating power from ocean waves and tides.

4. What does Peter Harper mean when he says wind is an "honest" energy choice (sidebar)?

Chapter 5: The Nuclear Option

1. Explain the basics of nuclear power production.

2. What are some of the primary arguments against increasing the use of nuclear power?

3. Why do some environmentalists say the risks from nuclear power are significantly less than the risks from fossil fuels?

4. Do you agree with Stewart Brand's opinion that it is fair to leave the burden of nuclear waste to future generations?

Chapter 6: The Future of Energy

1. What would be the pros and cons for a consumer when considering a purchase of green power? Why aren't more people purchasing green power?

2. Describe what the author means by an "efficiency paradox."

3. Do you think Americans are capable of a paradigm shift in energy attitudes?

4. How are consumers impacted by corporations' attention to alternative energy issues?

American Solar Energy Society (www.ases.org/)
2400 Central Avenue, Suite A
Boulder, CO 80301
(303) 443-3130
E-mail: ases@ases.org

This organization is devoted to the development of renewable energy. Their Web site includes a link to the online version of *Solar Today* magazine, with articles on advances in solar technology and other forms of alternative energy.

American Wind Energy Association (www.awea.org)
1101 Fourteenth Street NW, 12th Floor
Washington, DC 20005
(202) 383-2500
E-mail: windmail@awea.org

The AWEA provides information on all aspects of wind power. Its Web site contains a resource library with detailed fact sheets, articles, and answers to frequently asked questions.

Energy Information Administration (www.eia.doe.gov)
1000 Independence Ave. SW
Washington, DC 20585
(202) 586-8800
E-mail: InfoCtr@eia.doe.gov

This U.S. government agency offers a wide variety of energy-related information including information on both renewable and nonrenewable energy sources.

National Resources Defense Council (www.nrdc.org)
40 West 20th Street

New York, NY 10011
(212) 727-2700
E-mail: nrdcinfo@nrdc.org

The NRDC is an environmental action organization working on a variety of issues including oil dependence and global warming.

Nuclear Energy Institute (www.nei.org)
1776 I Street NW, Suite 400
Washington, DC 20006-3708
(202) 739-8000
E-mail: webmasterp@nei.org

The Nuclear Energy Institute is an organization supported by the nuclear energy industry. Their goal is the promotion of nuclear energy use in the United States and around the world.

Books and Periodicals

David Goodstein, *Out of Gas*. New York: Norton, 2004. The author outlines in understandable text his predictions of the future of energy in a world without fossil fuel.

Ian Graham, *Energy Forever? Fossil Fuels*. Austin, TX: Raintree Steck-Vaughn, 1999. This book provides an overview of the extraction and use of fossil fuels.

Wilborn Hampton, *Meltdown: A Race Against Nuclear Disaster at Three Mile Island*. Cambridge, MA: Candlewick, 2001. A reporter's eyewitness account of the unfolding events during the nuclear accident.

Nicole Bezic King, ed., *Renewable Energy Resources*. North Mankato, MN: Smart Apple Media, 2004. An examination of a variety of alternative energy sources.

Daniel A. Leone, ed., *Is the World Heading Toward an Energy Crisis*? Detroit: Greenhaven, 2006. This book presents varying opinions on questions relating to oil use and alternative energy sources.

Ewan McLeish, *21st Century Debates: Energy Resources*. Austin, TX: Raintree Steck-Vaughn, 2002. This book provides both facts and viewpoints concerning energy-related issues.

Sally Morgan, *Alternative Energy Sources*. Chicago: Heinemann, 2003. This book examines a variety of alternative energy technologies.

Time, "Special Report: Global Warming," April 3, 2006. A comprehensive look at the issues surrounding climate change.

Web Sites

Environmental Literacy Council (www.enviroliteracy.org). The Environmental Literacy Council is dedicated to helping students understand environmental issues. Their comprehensive Web site contains resources on almost every aspect of the natural world, including detailed information on energy issues.

Hydrogen Fuel Cells and Infrastructures Technology Program: Middle School Guide, U.S. Department of Energy (www.eere.energy.gov/hydrogenandfuelcells/education/middle_school.html). This U.S. government site offers a wide variety of information on fuel cells designed for middle school students, including a fuel cell overview, activity guide, Power Point presentations, and classroom poster.

Nuclear Energy Institute (www.nei.org). This comprehensive site produced by the nuclear power industry includes information on nuclear technology as well as safety and environmental issues.

Renewable Energy Basics, Union of Concerned Scientists (www.ucsusa.org/clean_energy/renewable_energy_basics/). This site describes different renewable energy sources including biofuels, as well as the environmental issues surrounding energy use.

U.S. Department of Energy, Energy Efficiency and Renewable Energy (www.eere.energy.gov/). This government site provides detailed information on clean energy sources such as solar, wind, biofuels, and fuel cells.

INDEX

PICTURE CREDITS

Cover, © iStockphoto.com/Stas Volik

AP Images, 16, 18, 21, 24, 27, 28, 30, 33, 35, 37, 39, 48, 51, 56, 60, 67, 69, 72, 76, 77, 80, 83, 87, 90, 95

© Bettmann/CORBIS, 7, 9

© CORBIS, 75

© Svenja-Foto/zefa/CORBIS, 54

© Walter Geiersperger/CORBIS, 43

© Jacques Langevin/CORBIS SYGMA, 92

© Will and Deni McIntyre/CORBIS, 19

© Christopher Morris/CORBIS, 64

© Schott AG/Solargenix Energy/Handout/epa/CORBIS, 45

© Lara Solt/Dallas Morning News/CORBIS, 14

Discovery Channel Images/Getty Images, 61

U.S. Environmental Protection Agency, 8

Steve Zmina, 15, 32, 68

ABOUT THE AUTHOR

Karen D. Povey has spent her career as a conservation educator, working to instill an appreciation for wildlife and wild places in people of all ages. Karen makes her home in Gig Harbor, Washington, and presents live animal programs at Tacoma's Point Defiance Zoo & Aquarium. She has written many books on wildlife and the environment including *Leopards, The Condor, Life in a Swamp,* and *Biofuels.* Karen supports alternative energy by driving a hybrid car and purchasing green power through her local utility company.